SANTA CRUZ

HAGGADAH

a Passover Haggadah, Coloring Book, and Journal
For The Evolving Consciousness

writing, calligraphy and art direction:

KAREN G.R. ROEKARD

artistic interpretation and illustration

NINA PALEY

computer layout and aesthetics

PAULA BOTTONE SPENCER

THE HINENI CONSCIOUSNESS PRESS
Berkeley, California

Contents

A few Hebrew words are frequently used so I will mention and translate them here.

    a) HASHEM - literally means 'the name' and is used as one way to refer to God within the understanding of the Jewish people.

    b) Mitzrayim - the Hebrew name for the ancient Egypt; literally comes from the source word for 'the narrow place.'

    c) Chometz - usually is translated as 'leavened bread' and anything that is not considered to be 'Kosher for Passover.' It also comes from a source word for 'oppress.'

    d) Chassid - a person who is spiritually-related to one of a number of groups who first arose in 18th century Eastern Europe; often they are committed to chesed, to deeds of loving-kindness, (the meaning of the root word for chassid), and/or mysticism. Santa Cruz, and Berkeley, the 'holy city to the north,' are full of many modern, New Age, Jewish Spiritual Renewal, Reb Zalman or Reb Shlomo chassids. To quote Reb Zalman, we are 'post-denominational Jews.'

January 27th, 1992

INTRODUCTION

1) MY TRUTH RIGHT NOW:

It is from a place of awe, a place of grace and gratitude, that I am re-writing this paragraph for the First Edition of The Santa Cruz Haggadah. Last year, for the Private Edition, I was writing from a place of shock and pain as the Gulf War had just started. This year, I know that my behavior in putting out the haggadah was right. This year I am finding it much easier to trust. And my prayer is that HASHEM, that energy that is beyond my ability to explain, will continue to smile on this endeavor.

2) PSYCHO-SPIRITUAL BELIEFS - FOUNDATIONS OF THIS HAGGADAH:

In my Orthodox Jewish childhood, the Haggadahs that we used at our Passover Seders followed the prescribed text: my father led the Seder and did most of the reading thus following traditional practice. Once I had grasped the basic story line, it became boring. Through the years, the addition of Midrashim, of interpretations and legends, gave Passover Seders additional meaning. And yet I noticed that my connection to the Seder and to the concept of slavery was mainly through my mind and through my mouth.

Over the past 20 years, with the addition of the liberation and the feminist Haggadahs, a new and very exciting dimension was added. I could relate to the feminist struggle; I could relate to the anguish of Jews unable to practice their religion and to other countries wherein there was no political freedom. I noticed that in addition to my intellectual connection to the concept of Passover and the Passover Seder, I was also connected through my guts -- the space of my power, or powerlessness, whichever the case was at that point in time.

Then almost five years ago, a new dimension came through for me. Somehow, when I went to write the first version of this Haggadah, what came through was the desire to connect to Passover and to the Seder in a way that was more congruent with the way that I was seeking to connect with all facets of my life, namely from a place of heart and soul, from a growing awareness of the ways in which I "enslave" myself, from the perspective of an evolving consciousness.

What does the concept of an evolving consciousness mean? Many things, many facets; different things to different people. For me it started with a realization and an acknowledgment that the reality that has the greatest validity and the one which I had the most trouble facing, was the reality of my personal psycho-spiritual 'right now.' I had grown accustomed to being bombarded with other perspectives of 'right now' - political 'right now,' work/corporate 'right now,' sports 'right now.' I realized that if I died at that moment in my history, the most logical thing they could put on my tombstone would have been, "she had a great career." Somehow, that just didn't feel quite right.

The second facet in the evolution to my current consciousness was the awakened desire to connect with Truth, with what really was the reality of my life situation in the psycho-spiritual 'right now.' The most significant truth, I realized, was the requirement that I needed to own some measure of responsibility for both the aspects of my life that were working and the aspects of my life that were not working.

This was very hard to do. "You did ....it's all your/his/her fault," are very potent statements, as is "if only ....would change/were different." I believe that it is these statements and belief systems that enslaved me and enslave us, that allow distances to be built within and between us. What I was learning, was that I have to be willing to look at my role in the life that I have created. I learned that I have to be open and accepting of all parts of myself; that only when I accept myself, am I able to see and accept other people.

I started to work at acknowledging the truth of my 'right now'; I started to own responsibility for my part in my current reality. I then found that when I took the time to quiet my mind and to go inside my being and ask questions - maybe asking for help, or for guidance, or for understanding - then more often than not, I would hear an answer that was deeper and wiser than I could possibly have expected from within my usual brain functioning.

What I came to, probably pretty late in life, was that I was connecting to a source of wisdom that seemed far greater than myself, far deeper in it's sense of understanding, far wiser in its response to my questions. I realized that this was the connection people spoke of when they spoke of connecting in to one's 'higher power,' to God, to Universal Consciousness, to the ONE.

For the wandering and somewhat lost Jew that I was, the words of the most profound Jewish prayer came to me and I was able to understand the concept of 'The One,' in a different way. The prayer, the Shm'a goes: "Shm'a Yisroel, HASHEM Eloheynu, HASHEM Echod -- Hear Israel, The NAME is our God, The NAME is ONE." For me the concept of The One, could comfortably take me back to my Jewish roots and be referred to as HASHEM.

And when I went to rewrite the Haggadah after having had this realization, I was struck by the words, "In every generation it is your duty to look upon yourself as if you had gone forth from Egypt!!" The Hebrew name for the ancient Egypt was Mitzrayim; the word Mitzrayim comes from a root word with a meaning, "the narrow place." I interpreted this to mean that in this generation, in my generation, from within my evolving consciousness, it is my gift to be able to understand Mitzrayim and the sensibility of slavery by looking into the 'right now' of my life and seeing, feeling, and knowing the ways in which I enslave myself, the ways in which I keep myself in narrow places.

I realized that if I want to fulfill this Passover obligation of each generation looking at itself as if it had come out of slavery, then I could most effectively do this by looking into the ways in which I hold myself back from being the best me I can be. Then I can at least visualize what it would mean to come out from this narrow place of holding myself back.

I started to utilize the concept of 'chometz,' of the leavened bread which we are not allowed to 'eat' during the days of Passover, as a symbol of those actions I take which do harm to my being, as those belief systems I have that hold me back, as those thoughts which put me down. Thus, to obey this commandment which disallows chometz for the duration of Passover, I decided to work to identify my 'chometz' each year and then to do my best to notice when I am 'eating' it. Success at this endeavor, in even some small way, has allowed the very significant psycho-spiritual healing modality of 'pattern disruption' to come into play for me.

Pattern disruption, making even the smallest change in any of my patterns of behavior or thoughts or beliefs, has consistently brought about a domino effect of change throughout my life. I learned that once I was willing to own my part in the actuality of my life, pattern disruption kept happening as quickly or as slowly as I allowed. It would happen through uncontrollable external events that would shake me. And when they happened, if I behaved from a 'conscious' place, a place wherein I would choose to see the event with the eyes of "I" and own responsibility, rather than through eyes that saw "You..." and ascribed blame, I knew I was supporting the evolution of my consciousness.

Pattern disruptions also kept happening through actions I chose to take -- like getting in touch with what I really want and asking for it; doing what I could to make it happen and then surrendering, letting go, and just trusting that what would be would be and that there was nothing more I could do. Disrupting my patterns and seeing what emerged was what became important.

Disrupting my patterns and still owning myself. Disrupting my patterns and owning my intelligence. Disrupting my patterns and owning my power. Disrupting my patterns and owning my heart. Disrupting my patterns and owning all parts of my being, even the parts I don't like. Taking the time to see, hear and feel my Truth and then looking for interconnection among all the parts.

Asking my mind: "Mind what truth do you think?" Listening to the answer and asking again.

"Guts what truth do you know?" and listening.

"Heart what truth do you feel?" and feeling the words of my heart.

"Genitals what truth do you know here?" and seeing what comes.

"Soul, Higher Power, what is real?" and letting the energy of an integrated answer come through.

Thus it was with overwhelming joy that I found within Judaism, the religion into which I had been born, a yearly ritual that prescribes it as our duty in each generation to find a way to put ourselves into a place of understanding of what it felt like to be enslaved in Mitzrayim, the ancient Egypt, and then to be freed; to know and to feel slavery. I find it wonderful that I am required to spend eight days wherein I am not allowed to eat "chometz," that which I have interpreted to be the patterns I manifest that hold me back, that keep me down. And then it feeds my soul to feel the support of a higher power, of the One, of HASHEM as HASHEM comes through me.

So how does this all fit in to this Haggadah? It is what this Haggadah is all about. It is about disrupting our patterns so that we can:

(a) connect with our Mitzrayim and our Chometz -- the ways in which we hold ourselves back from being the best version of ourselves that we can be;

(b) open our eyes and our hearts and see the truth of our present reality, our 'right now' and own our part in it, rather than ascribe blame;

(c) utilize our truth to acknowledge our needs and then ask for whatever it is that we need and want -- the ways we would like our reality to become, the parts of our beings we want to have reintegrated, our consciousness' to shift;

(d) take the actions that need to be taken to ensure that we have also done our 'active' part in creating our reality --"God helps those who help themselves;" and finally,

(e) enter into the state of grace, the place of trust and let go, of hoping that the 'ruach haKadosh,' the breath of Holy, will flow over, around and through us, knowing that what will be, will be, and that we cannot push the river.

I invite you to join me in this endeavor.

THE BIBLICAL INJUNCTION TO CELEBRATE PASSOVER:

If possible, read the Hebrew and the English text slowly, and simultaneously.

1   "And this day shall be unto you for a
memorial; and ye shall keep it a feast to
the Lord throughout your generations; ye
shall keep it a feast by an ordinance.
Seven days shall ye eat unleavened
bread; even the first day ye shall have put
away leaven out of your houses: for who-
soever eateth leavened bread from the
first day until the seventh day, that soul
shall feel cut off from Israel."

וְהָיָה הַיּוֹם הַזֶּה לָכֶם
לְזִכָּרוֹן וְחַגֹּתֶם אֹתוֹ חַג
לַיהֹוָה לְדֹרֹתֵיכֶם חֻקַּת
עוֹלָם תְּחָגֻּהוּ שִׁבְעַת
יָמִים מַצּוֹת תֹּאכֵלוּ אַף
בַּיּוֹם הָרִאשׁוֹן תַּשְׁבִּיתוּ
שְּׂאֹר מִבָּתֵּיכֶם כִּי כָּל
אֹכֵל חָמֵץ וְנִכְרְתָה הַנֶּפֶשׁ
הַהִוא מִיִּשְׂרָאֵל מִיּוֹם
הָרִאשׁוֹן עַד־יוֹם הַשְּׁבִיעִי:

(Exodus, XII, 14 - 15)

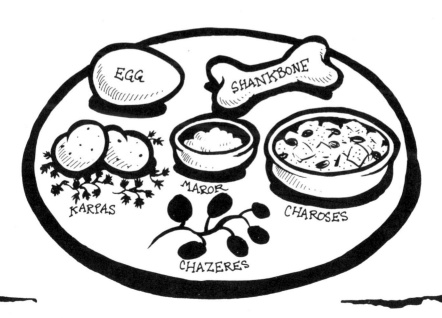

1 **CANDLE LIGHTING:**   Leader: We begin this
                                                            Passover Seder
celebration, as we begin all celebrations, by honoring Light - both the light
brought to us by candles and the light that we feel from all of the living
creatures in our lives.

2 As I read this meditation, let the Shammos candle, the Guiding Light candle,
be passed, from person to person, all around the room, each person lighting
a candle. Bring the light and the energy of the candles into and through you
by making three circles with your arms - from the candles back to your face -
and then cover your eyes with your hands.

Allow your mind's eye to see those whom you love who are not here. Invite
them to join us at this Seder.

3 **WE LIGHT THESE CANDLES:**

For our families, our beloveds, our friends, our animals -- for all our
relations;

For those who are no longer friends and for those who are no longer
enemies; for those from whom we feel an unwanted distance;

For those whose lives have been Touched and for those still awaiting
The Touch; for those who allow themselves to be seen and for those still
hiding out;

For all those who stay "a part of" and for those who have a need to
stay "apart from"; for all the wounded children;

For those who feel empty and for those who feel full; for those who confuse "more" and "enough;"

For those for whom it is easier to think of themselves and may yet learn to think of others; for those who can think of others but do not yet think of themselves;

For those just being born and for those who feel that they are old but have not yet been born; for those who feel as if they have never really lived;

For those in touch with their bodies who are getting in touch with their minds; for those in touch with their minds who are getting in touch with their bodies;

For those who can love and for those who have yet to learn to love; for those who have yet to learn to allow themselves to be loved;

For those who are getting what they want and for those who are getting what they need; for those who are not getting what they want or need; for those who do not yet know that they are getting what they want and what they need.

FOR EACH OF THESE WE LIGHT A CANDLE.

1   **Together let us sing or speak the prayer for the lighting of candles:**

בָּרוּךְ אַתָּה יְיָ אֱלֹהֵנוּ מֶלֶךְ הָעוֹלָם

2   Ba-ruch ahta HASHEM, e-lo-haynu melech ha-olam,

אֲשֶׁר קִדְּשָׁנוּ בְּמִצְוֹתָיו וְצִוָּנוּ

asher kid-shanu bi-mitz-vo-tav, vi-tzivanu,

לְהַדְלִיק נֵר שֶׁל יוֹם טוֹב:

li'hadlik ner shel yom tov.

4

1 Blessed is HASHEM, the Oneness, the Creator, Definer, Designer of the Universe, who has allowed us to find holiness through action, and has let it be known to us that through celebrating the creation of Light, we would begin to enter into the spirit of sacred days. Thus we light these candles.

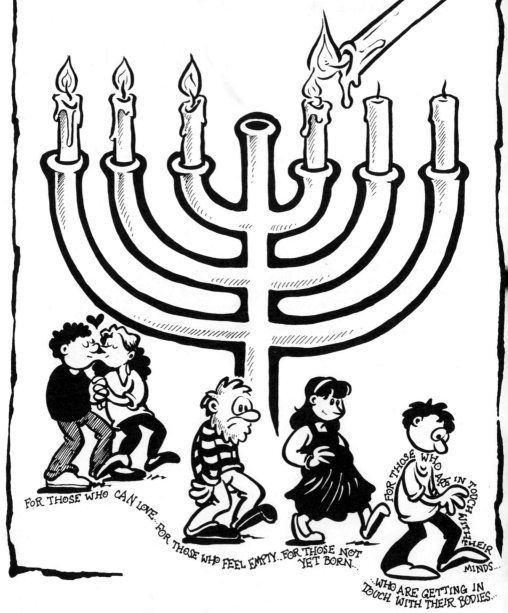

FOR THOSE WHO CAN LOVE...FOR THOSE WHO FEEL EMPTY...FOR THOSE NOT YET BORN...FOR THOSE WHO ARE IN TOUCH WITH THEIR MINDS... WHO ARE GETTING IN TOUCH WITH THEIR BODIES...

THE OPENING CHANTS:

At the beginning of religious activities, it is customary among Jewish mystics to chant expressions of their desire and their readiness to perform the prescribed rites. This tradition has been adopted by many Jews as yet another way of preparing their Neshamot, their souls, to make the shift from secular and mundane realities into sacred space.

The first chant, the Hinninee Moochon, is a chant of readiness. The Kadesh chant that follows, provides us with the complete order of activities at the Passover Seder.

הִנְנִי מוּכָן
וּמְזֻמָּן

Hinninee moo-chon oo-mizu-man

הִנְנִי מוּכָן וּמְזֻמָּן

Hinninee moochon oomizuman

הִנְנִי מוּכָן וּמְזֻמָּן

Hinninee moochon oomizuman

לְקַיֵּם מִצְוַת פֶּסַח:

Likah-yae-aim mitz-va-at Pesach

Here am I ready to fulfill(3)
The mitzvot of Pesach

6 THE ORDER OF THE SEDER:

קַדֵּשׁ	וּרְחַץ	כַּרְפַּס
KADESH	**U'RECHATZ**	**KARPAS**
the	*hand*	*fruit of*
sanctification	*washing*	*the earth*
יַחַץ	מַגִּיד	רָחַץ
YACHATZ	**MAGGID**	**RACHTZAH**
breaking of	*the story*	*hand washing*
the middle		*before eating*
matzah		
מוֹצִיא	מַצָּה	מָרוֹר
MOETZEE	**MATZAH**	**MAROR**
blessing over	*blessing for*	*bitter herbs*
bread	*matzah*	
כּוֹרֵךְ	שֻׁלְחָן עוֹרֵךְ	צָפוּן
KORECH	**SHULCHAN ARUCH**	**TZAFFON**
combination	*eating*	*eating the*
of matzah,	*the meal*	*afikoman*
maror, &		
charoset		
בָּרֵךְ	הַלֵּל	נִרְצָה
BARECH	**HALLEL**	**NIRTZAH**
recitation of	*giving praise*	*request for*
thanks after		*acceptance*
the meal		*of prayers*

KADESH

the sanctification

קַדֵּשׁ

1. Passover in its most obvious interpretation, is a celebration of the liberation of the Israelite people from their bondage in Mitzrayim, the ancient Egypt. Passover at its essence is a celebration of the great mystery of HASHEM as it flows through us and around us: the power of oneness and of wholeness, the truth of the physical and psycho-spiritual liberation that comes to those who acknowledge **WHAT IS,** and then **ASK** and **DO** and **LET GO** and **TRUST.**

Ba-ya-mim ha-hem, ba-zi-man ha-zeh

The events that we strive to recall were true for our ancestors in those times, as they are true for us in these times.

בַּיָּמִים הָהֵם בַּזְּמַן הַזֶּה

2. Our bodies were slaves in Mitzrayim, Bayamim Hahem, in those days, and there may be ways in which we feel as if our physical beings are entrapped now, Ba Ziman Hazeh, in a place where we do not want to be: maybe a city or a job or a relationship that doesn't feel right anymore; maybe an illness or a political situation or a style of life.

3. Our souls were trapped in Mitzrayim, Bayamim Hahem, in bodies that were enslaved. And it may be that Ba Ziman Hazeh our souls feel entrapped: maybe by our belief systems or by a need to project blame or by the parts of ourselves that we have not yet integrated: maybe an angry part or a jealous part, or a hurt child part or a part that feels controlled or controlling.

1.   And each of us knows our own internal soul reality; each of us knows what our own, personal, body-soul place of bondage, our Mitzrayim, looks like. Each of us knows the ways in which we enslave ourselves, our Chometz. Each of us knows the places in our lives and the parts of our being wherein we would like to have more freedom, more choices. Thus we can have some sense of knowing, Ba Ziman Hazeh, right now, what slavery feels like, even if we have never defined it to ourselves in this way.

2.   Each of us can evolve to a place of Acknowledging What Is and of Asking For Guidance and then Doing and Letting Go and Trusting in HASHEM, in the One, in wholeness. And each of us can then emerge from our own, self-generated Mitzrayim, as beings with greater freedom of body and greater freedom of soul.

3.   **TOGETHER:**
Let us remember,
for now and for all time,
that freedom starts
in our hands,
in our hearts,
in our minds,
with our internal reality.

Let us remember that
freedom begins
with acknowledging what is
and then choosing to be free,
taking actions to become free,
to feel free,
to allow freedom
and harmony
into our lives.

4.   Leader: *(Read Slowly)* Take a few minutes to relax and to orient yourself to your heart and to the voice of your truth, a voice that can only be heard from within. Look to become better acquainted with the ways in which you enslave yourself, your "Chometz", and with the parts of yourself that seem enslaved but whose bonds on your heart, you would like to loosen or to shift.

5.   *Song: RETURN AGAIN by Reb Shlomo Carlebach*

Return again, return again,
return to the land of your Soul.
(2X)

Return to WHO you are,
Return to WHAT you are,
Return to WHERE you are,
Born and reborn again.

1 **DRINKING THE FIRST CUP OF WINE**

To show that we are a free people, we pour the four cups of wine for each other, no one pouring his or her own cup. *Fill each other's cups now with the first cup of wine and then lift them up and all speak:*

2 **We sanctify this gathering with this first cup of wine.**

בָּרוּךְ אַתָּה יְיָ אֱלֹהֵינוּ מֶלֶךְ הָעוֹלָם

3 Baruch ahta HASHEM, elohaynu, melech ha-o-lam,

בּוֹרֵא פְּרִי הַגָּפֶן:

bo-ray pree ha-ga-fen.

4 **We are thankful to you, Maker of the Universe, for having created the fruit of the vine, this first cup of Passover wine, the cup of acknowledgment of what the truth IS in our lives right now. We acknowledge the parts of our being, both physical and spiritual, that want to trust in the power of HASHEM to create the wholeness where now exists Mitzrayim, the narrow place.**

בָּרוּךְ אַתָּה יְיָ אֱלֹהֵינוּ מֶלֶךְ הָעוֹלָם

5 Baruch ahta HASHEM, elohaynu melech ha-o-lam,

שֶׁהֶחֱיָנוּ וְקִיְּמָנוּ

sheh-heh-chayanu v'ki-yi-manu,

וְהִגִּיעָנוּ לַזְּמַן הַזֶּה:

v'he-geyanu la-zman ha-zeh.

6 **Blessed are you HASHEM, Creator of the universe, who has breathed life energy into us, who has provided us with the experiences that have made us who we are, and who has enabled us to reach this time in our lives.** *Drink the first cup of wine.*

U'RECHATZ: וּרְחַץ

hand washing

1
Rechatz.
The cleansing power of water.
Moisture.
The essence of life,
the flow of life.
Washing away hurts,
ways of thinking,
ways of being,
the things we want to let go of right now.
Allowing through that which has yet to emerge.
Making the way
for sacred space.

Fill a jug with water and bring it and an empty bowl to the table.

2 **One at a time, pour water over each others hands. As water is poured over your hands, share with us what you would like to let go of right now, what you would like to have "washed away." And after each person speaks, give them support by saying,** Kayn Yihee Ratzon **or "So Be It."**

KARPAS:

fruit of the earth

כַּרְפַּס

1

Karpas.
Honoring the physical supports.
Honoring the Earth, the solid part, the core.
Honoring growth from seed inspiration to fruition.
The blessings of the union
between what we can see and feel
with our naked eye,
and what we can only truly understand
with our naked soul.
Earth's lovemaking with the sun
with the rain,
with the ultimate mystery of HASHEM.
Food for the body, energy for the soul.
Sustenance, nourishment.
&
Salted Water.
The moisture of birth.
The pain of birth.
The tears at new beginnings.

2 *With our hands, we each choose a piece of Karpas, hold it up and say:*

בָּרוּךְ אַתָּה יְיָ אֱלֹהֵינוּ מֶלֶךְ הָעוֹלָם

3

Baruch ahta HASHEM, elohaynu melech ha-olam,

בּוֹרֵא פְּרִי הָאֲדָמָה:

bo-ray pree ha-a-da-mah.

4 **We thank you HASHEM, Maker of the universe, Mother Earth, for having created the fruits, the vegetables, the silent sustenance. We thank you for providing us with the support and the nourishment required in births and new beginnings.**

5 *Dip the Karpas in the salt water and eat it.*

YACHATZ:

יחץ

breaking of the middle matzah

1

Yachatz:
we halve the middle matzah.
The smaller portion becomes our Lechem Oe-nee.
The larger portion, we wrap in a napkin;
it is our Afikoman.

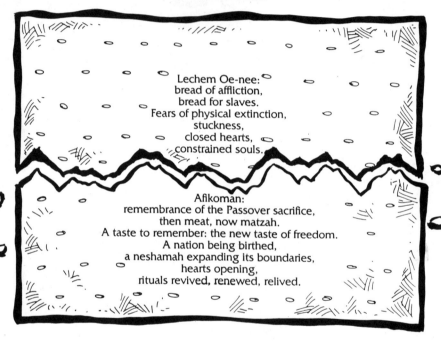

Lechem Oe-nee:
bread of affliction,
bread for slaves.
Fears of physical extinction,
stuckness,
closed hearts,
constrained souls.

Afikoman:
remembrance of the Passover sacrifice,
then meat, now matzah.
A taste to remember: the new taste of freedom.
A nation being birthed,
a neshamah expanding its boundaries,
hearts opening,
rituals revived, renewed, relived.

4   *Each child, starting with the older children and finishing with the younger children, takes a turn at putting the Afikoman on one of their shoulders while walking over to an adult participant and saying:*

"In haste we went out of Mitzrayim."

And that adult then responds:

"It is true; in haste we went out of Mitzrayim."

5   *The last adult to be approached by a child must hide the Afikoman during the meal. The children have the responsibility of finding it before the beginning of the second half of the Seder. The child who finds the Afikoman is entitled to a special present.*

1 **HA LACHMA ANYA:**

The Lechem Oenee half of the broken matzah is lifted and we chant the following three times:

הָא לַחְמָא עַנְיָא דִי אֲכָלוּ אַבְהָתָנָא
בְּאַרְעָא דְמִצְרָיִם.

2 Ha lach-ma anya, di-a-chalu av-hatanya, b'ara d'mitzrayim. (2)

כָּל דִכְפִין יֵיתֵי וְיֵכוֹל. כָּל דִּצְרִיךְ
יֵיתֵי וְיִפְסַח.

Kol dich-feen yetey v'yechvol; kol ditz-reech yetey v'yifsakh. (2)

הָשַׁתָּא הָכָא לְשָׁנָה הַבָּאָה בְּאַרְעָא
דְיִשְׂרָאֵל.

Ha-shatah ha-chah, l'shanah ha-ba-ah, bi-ara d'yisroel.

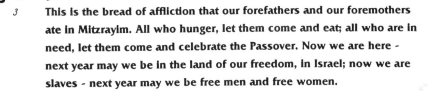

הָשַׁתָּא עַבְדֵי לְשָׁנָה הַבָּאָה
בְּנֵי חוֹרִין.

Ha-shatah av-dai, l'shanah ha-ba-ah, bi-nai choe-rin.

3 **This is the bread of affliction that our forefathers and our foremothers
ate in Mitzrayim. All who hunger, let them come and eat; all who are in
need, let them come and celebrate the Passover. Now we are here -
next year may we be in the land of our freedom, in Israel; now we are
slaves - next year may we be free men and free women.**

4 *Take a few minutes or as long as is comfortable to send loving energy to all who are poor, hungry, displaced,
oppressed or in the middle of a political conflict. Invite them to join us at our Seder.*

14

MAGGID:

the four questions

בַּגִּיד

1. *The second cup of wine is poured and The Four Questions are asked.* It is customary for a person who is a child in body, a child to the tradition, or young in spirit to ask the questions and for all of the participants to repeat each question after it has been asked. It is desirable that everyone ask questions throughout the Seder.

מַה נִּשְׁתַּנָּה הַלַּיְלָה הַזֶּה מִכָּל-הַלֵּילוֹת?

2. Ma nish-ta-nah ha-lie-la ha-zeh mee-kol ha-lay-lot?

שֶׁבְּכָל הַלֵּילוֹת אָנוּ אוֹכְלִין חָמֵץ

Sheh-b'chol ha-lay-lot ah-nu och-leen cha-maytz

וּמַצָּה הַלַּיְלָה הַזֶּה כֻּלּוֹ מַצָּה.

u-matzah; ha-lai-la ha-zeh, ku-lo matzah.

**How does this night differ from all other nights?
On all other nights we eat leavened and unleavened bread; on this
night, only matzah, unleavened bread.**

שֶׁבְּכָל הַלֵּילוֹת אָנוּ אוֹכְלִין שְׁאָר

3. Sheh-bi-chol ha-lay-lot ah-nu o'ch-leen shi-ar

יְרָקוֹת הַלַּיְלָה הַזֶּה מָרוֹר.

yi-ra-kot; ha-lei-la ha-zeh, maror.

**On all other nights we eat all manner of herbs;
on this night, only those that are bitter.**

שֶׁבְּכָל הַלֵּילוֹת אֵין אָנוּ מַטְבִּילִין אֲפִילוּ

4. Sheh-bi-chol ha-lay-lot ayn ah-nu mot-bee-leen ah-feelu

פַּעַם אֶחָת הַלַּיְלָה הַזֶּה שְׁתֵּי פְעָמִים.

p'ahm e-chot; ha-lei-la ha-zeh, sh'tay pi-ah-meem.

**On all other nights we do not steep that which
we eat even once; on this night, twice.**

שֶׁבְּכָל הַלֵּילוֹת אָנוּ אוֹכְלִין

1 Sheh-bi-chol ha-lay-lot ah-nu oh-chleen

בֵּין יוֹשְׁבִין וּבֵין מְסֻבִּין

bayn yosh-veen ooh-vayn mi-su-been;

הַלַּיְלָה הַזֶּה כֻּלָנוּ מְסֻבִּין

ha-lei-lah ha-zeh ku-lanu mi-su-been.

On all other nights, we eat either sitting or reclining; on this night, all recline.

Another Four Questions:

2 Why is it that with all the work we have done on ourselves, there are still ways in which we feel unfree, ways in which we constrain ourselves?

3 Why is it that with all our self-knowledge, there is still so much misunderstanding between parent and child, husband and wife, lover and beloved, employer and employee, friend and friend?

4 Why is it that with all that we know about conflict resolution there are still wars between nations, there are still children going to war, there are still innocent people dying?

5 Why is it that with all that we know about our inter-relationship with our planet, we still allow ourselves and others to dishonor her through one of a million detrimental actions?

6 What are some other questions you have?

MAGGID

the recitation:

עֲבָדִים הָיִינוּ לְפַרְעֹה בְּמִצְרָיִם:

1 Avadim ha-yeenu li-Paroh bi-Mitzrayim: **We were slaves to Pharaoh in Mitzrayim. We saw the boundaries of his world, the land of Mitzrayim, as the whole of the world. And from within that world, from within that context, Pharaoh was God and we were the lowliest of living creatures; from within that world, none had ever escaped.**

וַיוֹצִיאֵנוּ יְיָ אֱלֹהֵינוּ מִשָּׁם:

2 Va-yoe-tziyenu HASHEM eloheynu me-shom: **We were taken out of there, we were released, we were shown the way, we were brought to the next stage of our evolution through our cries for help and our trust in HASHEM, our Maker.**

3 **And if the Holy ONE, if HASHEM, had not chosen to redeem our ancestors from their Mitzrayim, and if they had not surrendered to the mystery of HASHEM's will at that time, then we, and our children and our children's children would still be enslaved to the reality and/or the beliefs of a Pharaoh in a Mitzrayim.**

Another reply:

עֲבָדִים הָיִינוּ לְפַרְעֹה בְּמִצְרָיִם.

1   Avadim ha-yeenu li-Paroh bi-Mitzrayim: **Sometimes we see our lives only from within the narrow context, the Mitzrayim, within which we live; and from within this self-generated version of reality, we lose sight of alternative possibilities, we see no avenue of change; we see only "Mitzrayim."**

וַיּוֹצִיאֵנוּ יְיָ אֱלֹהֵינוּ מִשָּׁם

2   Va-yoe-tziyenu HASHEM eloheynu me-shom: **And it is only when we acknowledge the truth of our lives, and surrender to a trust in HASHEM, it is only then that a myriad of possibilities for evolution begin to appear. It is only when we can say, "I don't know and I need help," that all the magical mystery forces of HASHEM in the Universe come forth to give us the answers that guide our way out of our Mitzrayim.**

3   And until we choose to surrender ourselves to the mystery of HASHEM's will, to the healing power of asking, doing, and trusting, then we and our children and our children's children will be enslaved to our inherited or self-created Mitzrayims of the Soul.

18

Song:
<u>Amazing Grace</u>
as interpreted
by Max Samson   and David Maleckar

Amazing
Grace,
how sweet
the sound
that saved
a soul
like me.
I once was lost
but now I'm found,
was blind but now I see.

Once enslaved
by wretched pride
I'd take a part of me
I did not want
inside myself
And build an enemy.

Knowing I
was once oppressed,
believing myself free,
In darkness
I saw only this --
the Moses side of me.

Amazing Grace,
how bright the light
that made my eyes to see,
My shadow
cast upon the wall,
the Pharaoh side of me.

For every light
there is a dark,
two halves that make a soul,
We must embrace
the paradox,
to make our spirit whole.

Amazing Grace,
how sweet the sound
that saved a soul like me.
I once was lost
but now I'm found,
was blind but now I see.

וַאֲפִילוּ כֻּלָּנוּ חֲכָמִים

1. Vi-afeelu koolanu chachamim: **And even if we are people who see ourselves as "smart"-- as persons who already know the facts and the details; even then we are still obliged to tell the story of the departure from Mitzrayim.**

כֻּלָּנוּ נְבוֹנִים

2. Koolanu nivoneem: **And if we are people who see ourselves as "wise," as people who already have spiritual knowingness and understanding; even then, we are still obliged to tell the story of the departure from Mitzrayim.**

כֻּלָּנוּ זְקֵנִים

3. Koolanu zikaynim: **And if we have attained to "old age;" even then we are still obliged to tell the story of the departure from Mitzrayim.**

כֻּלָּנוּ יוֹדְעִים אֶת הַתּוֹרָה

4. Koolanu yodim et ha'Torah: **And if we are "Knowers of the Torah", even then we are still obliged to tell the story of the departure from Mitzrayim.**

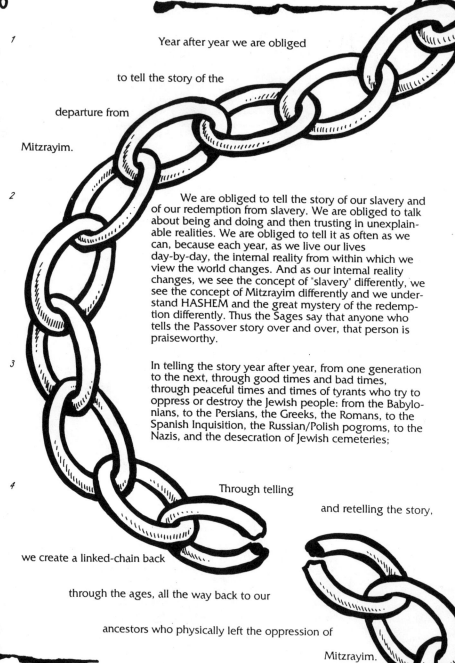

1

Year after year we are obliged

to tell the story of the

departure from

Mitzrayim.

2

We are obliged to tell the story of our slavery and of our redemption from slavery. We are obliged to talk about being and doing and then trusting in unexplainable realities. We are obliged to tell it as often as we can, because each year, as we live our lives day-by-day, the internal reality from within which we view the world changes. And as our internal reality changes, we see the concept of "slavery" differently, we see the concept of Mitzrayim differently and we understand HASHEM and the great mystery of the redemption differently. Thus the Sages say that anyone who tells the Passover story over and over, that person is praiseworthy.

3

In telling the story year after year, from one generation to the next, through good times and bad times, through peaceful times and times of tyrants who try to oppress or destroy the Jewish people: from the Babylonians, to the Persians, the Greeks, the Romans, to the Spanish Inquisition, the Russian/Polish pogroms, to the Nazis, and the desecration of Jewish cemeteries;

4

Through telling

and retelling the story,

we create a linked-chain back

through the ages, all the way back to our

ancestors who physically left the oppression of

Mitzrayim.

THE FOUR CHILDREN:

1

Pharaoh tried to destroy the future
by killing the bodies of the children.
He failed.
Others destroy the future
by killing the souls of the children.
Sometimes they succeed; sometimes they fail.
We honor the children.
All Children.
Children who sit in front of us - the future;
Child-parts that live inside us - the past.

2

Four kinds of children, four sets of child-parts.
Four different perspectives:
seeing things, feelings things, hearing things,
knowing things, differently.
Each to be respected.
Each to be told the story in a way that allows it to be open to learn.

אֶחָד חָכָם

3 **The WISE Child/The WISE-Child Part: the mature curiosity and open
mind-heart that asks, "What are the Passover activities all about?" This
child/child part should be taught to perform the specific actions of
Passover celebration and then given an opportunity to share and create
personally meaningful rituals. This child should be told about the many
types of Mitzrayim there are in life and about ways to move into
liberation.**

22

וְאֶחָד רָשָׁע

1   The CYNICAL Child/The CYNICAL-Child Part isolates and manifests anger and a closed heart asking, "What is this service to you? this Passover?" This child/child part should be answered with patience and loving energy and an invitation to participate even if the feeling and the understanding are not there. For it is often in the "doing" that the feeling content is changed; it is often in the "doing" that the sense of being "a part of," becomes real.

וְאֶחָד תָּם

2   The INNOCENT Child/The INNOCENT-Child Part asks: "What is this? Why are we doing this?" This child/child part should be told facts, that we get together every year to celebrate a time long, long ago when HASHEM freed us from being slaves in a place called Mitzrayim.

וְאֶחָד שֶׁאֵינוֹ יוֹדֵעַ לִשְׁאוֹל

3   And the Children who are TOO YOUNG TO ASK we bring to a point of present awareness. We entertain them and show them what is in front of them, the unique things about the table: the Passover plate and its contents, the Matzot, and the fact that everyone is gathered. Then we ask them what they imagine from everything they see.

4   **THE STORY OF PASSOVER**   And now it is time to tell this story of a redemption: the liberation of the children of Israel from their oppressors at that moment in history 32 centuries or so ago. Like most stories, it has a seeming beginning, although we could always go back further and find a different beginning; the story could always be told from a different perspective and be a different story.

5   The choice in this Haggadah is to acknowledge the idea that our ancestors were idol worshippers but to start the story here with Joseph, the eleventh son and favored child of his father Jacob, the third of the three forefathers of the Jewish people. Joseph was a strong, self-possessed and provocative boy who was hated by his brothers. After he told them about a dream wherein the sun, the moon and the stars were bowing down to him, they decided that they had had enough of him and, unbeknownst to their father Jacob, they sold Joseph into slavery in Mitzrayim.

1   Through the wise use of his God-given gifts, he eventually rose to a position of minister to the Pharaoh. When a time of famine came, he was able to save the lives of his brothers and their families and he was able to forgive them. Thus came the children of Jacob, who was also known as Israel, to reside in Mitzrayim. What was supposed to have been a temporary sojourn became a semi-permanent residency. Time passed, Joseph died and a Pharaoh came to power who did not know of all that Joseph had done for the people and the rulers of Mitzrayim.

2   This Pharaoh feared the enlarged population and the enlarged might of the Israelites; he feared that in the event of bad times, they would rise up against him or side with his enemies. So he enslaved the Israelites and in that way controlled them. He had the desire to wipe them out, to rid his nation of this seeming "enemy from within" and so decreed that all male children should be killed at birth and only female children be allowed to live.

3   Through HASHEM's intervention, Moses, Mosheh, a male child, was spared. In the course of life's circumstances, he had to flee from Mitzrayim to Midian where he took a wife and created a family. During this time, the plight of the Children of Israel got worse and worse and reached the point of ultimate pain. They cried to HASHEM to free them from their misery. HASHEM came to Mosheh in a burning bush in the desert and told him that he, Mosheh, had been chosen to be HASHEM's intermediary on earth in the liberation of the Children of Israel from slavery.

4   Mosheh protested, citing all of his inadequacies, and especially his speech impediment. HASHEM insisted that Mosheh was to be the leader.

1   THE DRAMA OF THE PASSOVER STORY   by   Max Samson   and
                                                      David Maleckar

The Locale: Any narrow place, arid.
The Characters:
Pharaoh   Essentially a stubborn,
                    bossy type
Moses   Speech impaired leader
God   Gruff but lovable
The People   Slightly inebriated

Scene 1: The Wilderness

Moses:	Oh look, a burning buth.
God:	Behold, Moses.
Moses:	A talking burning buth.
God:	Put off thy shoes.
Moses:	A bothy, talking, burning buth.
God:	Go take my people out of bondage.
Moses:	Who am I to do thith great thing?
God:	I will be with you.
Moses:	Who are you, if anybody athkth.
God:	I am that I am.
Moses:	A yam? You're a yam?
God:	OK Mo, call me a yam but the next time you see me burning you better scram!
Moses:	A point well taken. See you at Pharaoh's palace.

Scene Two: The Palace

Moses:	Lithen Pharaoh, my people, like anybody elthe, don't mind working, but they hate being slaveth!
People: (in unison)	We don't mind working, cause we're no knaves; But don't be whippin' cause we hate being slaves!
Pharaoh:	Tough. Nothing personal but my heart's been hardened.
People: (in unison)	Unfeeling brute! Bounder! Cad! He won't listen, but he'll wish he had!
Moses:	God. Lithen. Pharaoh won't lithen. He won't do like you athked and let my people go.
People: (in unison)	You got to let that Pharaoh know, he got to let your people go!

1. Leader: Let us breathe for a moment and meditate on the "impediments," in our lives: on the physical handicaps with which we find ourselves "stuck;" on the external aspects of our lives that we believe hold us back; on the excuses we continue to make. Can you find a way to laugh at your own "impediments" as easily as you could laugh during this dramatization?

2. *A Song:*   *When Israel was in Egypt land,*
Let my people go.
Oppressed so hard they could not stand;
Let my people go.

Chorus:

Go down, Moses, way down in Egypt land;
Tell old Pharaoh to "Let my people go!"
We need not always weep and mourn,
Let my people go.
And wear these chains of slaves forlorn,
Let my people go.

Chorus:

No more shall they in bondage toil,
Let my people go;
Let them come out with Egypt's spoil,
Let my people go.

Chorus:

3. וַיּוֹצִיאֵנוּ יְיָ מִמִּצְרַיִם בְּיָד חֲזָקָה

Vayoe-tzee-aynu HASHEM me-Mitzrayim bi-yad chazakah,

וּבִזְרוֹעַ נְטוּיָה וּבְמוֹרָא גָּדוֹל

ooh-vih-zroah ni-too-yah, ooh-vi-moe-rah gahdol

וּבְאֹתוֹת וּבְמוֹפְתִים:

ooh-vih-oh-tut ooh-vih-moaf-teem.

4. "And HASHEM took us out of Mitzrayim with a mighty hand, with an outstretched arm, with great fearsomeness and with signs and wonders." (Exodus 26:8)

5. Pharaoh, in spite of all the miracles presented to him, would not believe that the force of the Israelite God was powerful enough to insist that he free the children of Israel from their slavery.

1   HASHEM sent ten plagues on the people of Mitzrayim. With each plague, while it was happening, Pharaoh would give in; and when each plague ceased, Pharaoh's heart 'hardened' and he withdrew his willingness to let the Israelites go. It was only with the tenth plague, the killing of the firstborn sons of the Mitzrayim households, that Pharaoh let the Israelites go.

2   It is customary to call out the listing of plagues and to recall that each plague related to some aspect of the Israelite slavery. In the same way, each problematic situation in which we find ourselves, the 'plagues' in our lives, relate to some way in which we enslave ourselves, some lesson we still have to learn.

3   As each plague is listed, we put a utensil or a finger into our wine cups and drop a drop of wine from it. We do this to remember the fact that with the liberation of the Israelites came tremendous suffering and loss on the part of the people of Mitzrayim. Thus we take drops from our wine so as to reduce our pleasure.

4   **DOM**
The turning of the Nile's waters into **BLOOD** -- the response to the shedding of Israelite BLOOD.

דָּם

5   **TZIFAARDAYAH**
The invasion of **FROGS** -- the response to forcing the Israelites to load Egyptian freight which the FROGS then destroyed.

צְפַרְדֵעַ

6   **KEENIM**
The invasion of **LICE** -- the response to having to use earth to make clay and bricks. The earth then turned into LICE.

כִּנִּים

1 **AHROVE**
The invasion of
WILD BEASTS --
the response to the
Israelites having to
gather all kinds of
animals for use by
their task masters.
During this plague,
the BEASTS
attacked the
humans.

עָרוֹב

2 **DEHVER**
The killing of the
cattle by **PESTI-
LENCE** -- the Isra-
elites had been
forced to tend the
herds of the Mitz-
rim and the PESTI-
LENCE now came
and killed the
herds.

דֶּבֶר

3 **SHICHEEN**
The bodies of the
Mitzrim became
covered with
BOILS -- the Israel-
ites were required
to draw the baths
of the Mitzrim. The
BOILS made it
impossible for
them to bathe.

שְׁחִין

4 **BAHRAHD**
The showering
with **HAILSTONES**
-- the Israelites
were forced to be
stonecutters in the
creation of the pyr-
amids. Thus came
the showering with
HAILSTONES.

בָּרָד

1. **AHRBEH**
The over-running of the country by **LOCUSTS** -- the Israelites were forced to tend the fields and vineyards of the Mitzrim and so their fields were destroyed by LOCUSTS.

אַרְבֶּה

2. **CHOSHECH**
The envelopment by **DARKNESS** -- because the Mitzrim darkened the lives of the Israelite slaves, they were now cursed with DARKNESS.

חֹשֶׁךְ

3. **MAKAT BICHOROT**
The killing of the **FIRSTBORN** -- The desire to wipe out the Israelites led to the final plague, the KILLING of the FIRSTBORN.

מַכַּת בְּכוֹרוֹת

4. **Rabbi Yehuda used to group them by their initials:**

DITZACH

דְּצַ"ךְ

ADASH

עֲדַ"שׁ

BI-AH-HAB

בְּאַחַ"ב

5. What do each of these plagues represent for us today? What are some of the plagues striking planet earth and her living creatures to which we are not yet fully responding? What can we do to avoid waiting until the "firstborn" are killed to acknowledge and do something about them?

1   **CHANTING OF**
VIHEE SHEH-AHMDAH

We grieve over the fact that horrors had to befall fellow living creatures in order for us to be liberated. At the same time though, we thank HASHEM for having taken the steps necessary to ensure that our liberation from Mitzrayim could occur.

2   **We lift our glasses of wine and chant the following.**

וְהִיא שֶׁעָמְדָה לַאֲבוֹתֵינוּ וְלָנוּ.

3   Vi-hee sheh-ahm-dah, vi-hee sheh-ahm-dah,
lah-voe-taynu vi-lah-nu.(2)

שֶׁלֹּא אֶחָד בִּלְבָד עָמַד עָלֵינוּ לְכַלּוֹתֵנוּ.

Sheh-lo eh-chad bil-vad, ah-mad ah-lay-nu,
li-chah-lo-tay-nu (2)

לְכַלּוֹתֵנוּ. אֶלָּא שֶׁבְּכָל דּוֹר וָדוֹר עוֹמְדִים עָלֵינוּ

Eh-lah sheh-bi-chol dore vah-dore,
ohm-dim alay-nu li-chah-low-tay-nu (2)

וְהַקָּדוֹשׁ בָּרוּךְ הוּא מַצִּילֵנוּ מִיָּדָם:

Vi-hah-kah-dush Bar-chu, mah-tziy-lay-nu mee-yah-dam.

4   And She stood up for our forebearers and for us. For it is not one alone who has stood up to destroy us. Rather, it is in every era and generation that there are those who stand up to destroy us. And the Holy One, the Blessed One, saves us from their hands.

THE LESSONS

There are many lessons that can be learned from this story. One of the major lessons for the Jewish people, has been the recognition that in every generation there have been nations or individuals who have seen the Jews as a strange, self-isolating group, as a potential enemy from within. And that leader or that country has tried to annihilate, to wipe out the Jews, either physically or spiritually. And in every generation, these self-styled oppressors fail.

2   A lesson for all persons might be that if you want liberation for an oppressed part of yourself, an oppressed part of your world, you have to determinedly want that liberation. You have to determinedly want anything and then you have to be flexible in your approach to getting it. And if the powers in the Universe, have ordained that it be so, then you have to be prepared to Ask and to Do and to Let Go and Trust and then to stand up and be knocked down, to stand up and be knocked down -- over and over and over again. And just as water finally wears down a path through even the toughest rock, if there is a path, if there is a way, if it is meant to be, it will manifest.

3   You also have to know the difference between "more" and "enough" (dayeanu). We always want more -- more freedoms, more love, more attention, more things, more knowledge, more playtime, more money, more... more... more... and we want it NOW!!! The Haggadah teaches us that each step along our paths must be acknowledged and celebrated as "enough." If there is "more" for our cups, then we are of the Blessed if we realize that it was not our "right", we did not have it "coming to us." Rather, it is a gift from the Universe, from HASHEM, and each time we get "more," HASHEM deserves a "thank you."

Song: DAYEANU

Chorus: Dai-dai-yea-nu, dai-dai-yea-nu,
dai-dai-yea-nu, dayeanu, dayeanu.

1

For how many good turns do we owe a thanks?

אִלּוּ הוֹצִיאָנוּ מִמִּצְרַיִם וְלֹא-עָשָׂה בָהֶם שְׁפָטִים

Eey-lu hoe-tze hoe-tze yah-nu, hoe-tze yah-nu me-mitz-ra-yim, vi-loh aah-sah
ba-hem shi-fa-teem.

Dayeanu   **Chorus**

2

**Had HASHEM brought us out of Mitzrayim,
and not wrought judgement on them, Dayeanu.**

אִלּוּ עָשָׂה בָהֶם שְׁפָטִים וְלֹא-עָשָׂה בֵאלֹהֵיהֶם

Eey-lu ah-sah ba-hem shi-fa-teem,
vi-loh aah-sah bay-ay-lo-hay-hem:

Dayeanu   **Chorus**

3

**Had HASHEM wrought judgement on them
but not on their gods, Dayeanu**

אִלּוּ עָשָׂה בֵאלֹהֵיהֶם וְלֹא-הָרַג אֶת בְּכוֹרֵיהֶם

Eey-lu ah-sah bay-lo-hay-hem,
vi-loh ha-rag et bi-cho-ray-hem,

Dayeanu   **Chorus**

4

**Had HASHEM wrought judgement on their Gods,
and not slain their firstborn, Dayeanu.**

5

Reader speak: **Had HASHEM slain their firstborn, and not given us their
wealth,**   *All respond:* **Dayeanu**

6

Reader: **Had HASHEM given us their wealth, and not divided the sea,**
All respond: **Dayeanu**

7

Reader: **Had HASHEM divided the sea, and not brought us through it on
dry land,**   *All respond:* **Dayeanu**

8

Reader: **Had HASHEM brought us through the sea on dry land and not
drowned our oppressors in it,**   *All respond:* **Dayeanu**

9

Reader: **Had HASHEM sunk our oppressors in it, and not sated our needs
in the desert forty years,**   *All respond:* **Dayeanu**

1 *Reader:* **Had HASHEM sated our needs in the desert forty years, and not fed us with Manna,**   *All respond:* **Dayeanu**

2 *Reader:* **Had HASHEM fed us with Manna, and not given us the Sabbath,**   *All respond:* **Dayeanu**

3 *Reader:* **Had HASHEM given us the Sabbath, and not brought us to Mount Sinai,**   *All respond:* **Dayeanu**

4 *Reader:* **Had HASHEM brought us to Mount Sinai and not given us the Torah,**   *All Respond:* **Dayeanu**

All Sing: Dai Dai Yea Nu .....

5 אִלּוּ נָתַן לָנוּ אֶת הַתּוֹרָה וְלֹא הִכְנִיסָנוּ לְאֶרֶץ יִשְׂרָאֵל

Eey-lu nah-tan lah-nu et ha-toe-rah, vi-loh hech-nee-sah-nu li-eretz yees-ro-el,

Dayeanu   **Chorus**

6 **Had HASHEM given us the Torah, and not led us into the Land of Israel, Dayeanu.**

7 אִלּוּ הִכְנִיסָנוּ לְאֶרֶץ יִשְׂרָאֵל וְלֹא בָנָה לָנוּ אֶת הַבְּחִירָה בֵּית

Eey-lu hech-nee-sah-nu li-e-retz yis-ro-el, vi-loh ba-nah et bayt ha-bih-chee-rah,

Dayeanu   **Chorus**

8 **Had HASHEM led us into the Land of Israel, and not built a Temple for us: Dayeanu**

Another perspective on DAYEANU:

1   If we could set the priority in our lives to worshiping HASHEM, to worshiping oneness and wholeness, rather than the gods of money, science, power and pleasure. Dayeanu

2   If we could remember that each of us is created in the image of HASHEM, if we could treat all living creatures, starting with ourselves, with the loving kindness warranted by being a manifestation of the spark of the Divine. Dayeanu

3   If we could only see how short and precious life is and take care of ourselves, without having to be reminded through tragedy or ill health. Dayeanu

4   If we could catch ourselves about to speak Loshen Horah, gossip and tale-bearing, and instead, choose to vocally acknowledge that which we usually take for granted. Dayeanu

5   If we could realize that when we do harm to our neighbors, friends, employees, parents, children, animals, or environment, we are doing spiritual, psychological, or physical harm to ourselves. Dayeanu

6   If we could learn to see each other as we really are as opposed to projecting memories or images of other people onto each other. Dayeanu

7   If we could then listen to each other when we share; if we could regularly feel heard and understood. Dayeanu

1   If we could make it a practice to spend time being with ourselves, honest about the truths of our lives, getting clear about what we want to learn or work on.
                                                                          Dayeanu

2   If we could give and receive all of the intimacy, affection, support, nurturance, and sex we need on an ongoing basis, to and from appropriate sources.
                                                                          Dayeanu

3   If we could have fulfilling work, exciting play, creative endeavors, and no boredom.
                                                                          Dayeanu

4   If the children of the world could receive the good-enough parenting, schooling, and feeding that would allow them to grow into healthy and stable adults.
                                                                          Dayeanu

5   If the fears of ill-health, loneliness and poverty could be dispelled so that aging would be seen as part of the process of living as opposed to being something to be feared.
                                                                          Dayeanu

6   If the commitment to lifetime learning, growth, risk-taking and expanded consciousness could become intense enough to allow for a critical mass of awakened, concerned and fully alive human beings to once again walk the planet at the same time.
                                                                          Dayeanu

7   If we could then see Tikkun Olam, universal healing, in our lifetimes.
                                                                          Dayeanu

8   If we could go out into the world and share the joyous message of the Haggadah and the redemption and the way we feel tonight celebrating Passover together.
                                                                          Dayeanu
                                                                          Dayeanu

9   *Leader: Take a few minutes to look inside and ask, what would be 'Dayeanu' for me this year?*

1 **THE SYMBOLS OF PASSOVER**

Rabbi Gamliel used to say that whoever has not explained the following three things at the Passover Seder has not fulfilled his duty:

PESACH, MATZAH, MAROR

→ VEGETARIAN Z'ROAH

2 **PESACH** פֶּסַח Z'roah. A roasted shankbone: Symbol of the Passover sacrifice eaten during the days of the Temple to honor the fact that HASHEM passed over the houses of the children of Israel in Mitzrayim while at the same time, striking down the firstborn of the houses of the Mitzrim.

3 Another interpretation: As HASHEM led the Israelites out of Mitzrayim, it was with Z'roah Nituyah - with a strong arm. This reminds us that in creating the paths of our personal evolutions, we must remember to include a strong support, a z'roah nituyah, a shoulder upon which we can lean, on whom we can depend.

MATZAH מַצָּה *(The Lechem Oenee half of the middle Matzah is lifted up for all to see)*

4 **This Matzah, which did not have the time to rise and become bread as we generally know it, this Matzah is a symbol of not being "ready" but of having to do something anyway!** We may not feel "ready" for liberation from our Mitzrayim of the Soul, from our unique form of "slavery." Sometimes though, we must "eat it" as it comes, accept it when it shows its face, do it even though we don't feel quite ready and then see what happens.

5 Sometimes it is in the "doing" that the "feeling" comes -- we do something and the first time it doesn't feel right at all; the second time it feels better, righter; the third time, it is easier still. By the fourth time, it is a part of us. Whenever we eat Matzah, may we remember the "doing" in addition to the "feeling."

MAROR בָּרוֹר *(The Maror is held up for all to see)*

1 This Maror is the symbol of the bitterness of servitude. It serves as a perpetual reminder, from generation to generation, that it is the duty of Jews, as the descendants of slaves, to do whatever can be done to lighten the load of those less fortunate and to have sympathy for all living creatures who are enslaved by virtue of their environment, their heredity or their own sense of lack of choice.

Reb Zalman Schachter-Shalomi reminds us that Maror is also meant to reawaken for us the pain and the bitterness that are sometimes a part of our lives. We go through the pain and we forget it; sometimes we learn from it, sometimes we don't. Maror with its harsh taste brings us, once again, to the reality of the pain.

בְּכָל דוֹר וָדוֹר חַיָּב אָדָם

2 Bi-chol dor va-dor chah-yav ah-dam

לִרְאוֹת אֶת עַצְמוֹ

leer-ot et atzmoe

3 **IN EVERY GENERATION,**

WE ARE OBLIGED TO REGARD OURSELVES

AS IF WE PERSONALLY

HAD BEEN LIBERATED FROM MITZRAYIM!!

כְּאִלוּ הוּא יָצָא מִמִּצְרַיִם

ki-eey-lu who yah-tzah me-mitrayim!!

1. According to Maaseh Nissim: On Passover eve, the spirit of liberation and redemption once again stirs in people's hearts. Our task is to make ourselves worthy of it by breaking out of the spiritual and physical shackles we allow to enslave us and once again, to give thanks.

2.

Therefore we are duty-bound
to acknowledge the splendor.
We are duty-bound
to praise,
to glorify,
to exalt,
and to hold high,
that Beingness
that performed these miracles
for our ancestors and for us:
for bringing us from bondage to freedom,
from sorrow to joy,
from days of mourning to days of holiday,
from darkness into the Light,
and from slavery to redemption.

3. **THE CALL TO
RECITE HALLEL**

And we will sing a new song, the song of the time of the Exodus. And then we too will feel the feelings of being redeemed, released, reawakened from the pain of bondage; the long years of enslavement to a nation with completely foreign ways, enslavement to that which does not feel related to our spiritual being.

4.
$$\text{וְנֹאמַר לְפָנָיו שִׁירָה חֲדָשָׁה:}$$

Vi-no-mar li-fah-nav she-rah cha-dasha:(4X)
HALLELEUYA!! (4X)

5. **And we should sing before HASHEM,
a new song:
Halleleuya!**

בְּצֵאת יִשְׂרָאֵל מִמִּצְרָיִם,

Bi-tzait Yisrael me-Miz-ra-yim

בֵּית יַעֲקֹב מֵעַם לֹעֵז:

beyt Yaakov, may-om lo-aize

When the light that is Yisrael
was able to emerge shining
from the darkness of Mitzrayim,
when the distinction between the house of Yaakov
and the peoples who spoke a completely foreign
spiritual language was made obvious,
then the Tribe of Yehudah
became consecrated in holiness,
and all of Yisrael
became the dominion of HASHEM.

The sea saw the change and divided,
the Jordan River turned around and changed course.
The mountains and the hills, in their awe,
moved and quaked and skipped
like rams and young lambs.

"What is with you sea that you divide?
Jordan, how do you change your course?
Mountains, why do you move and skip like rams?
You hills, like young lambs?"

"On account of the presence of HASHEM!
On account of the presence of the God of Jacob
who can transform boulders
into pools of standing waters,
and flint, into flowing streams of water!!"

Song: *Glory Halleleuya*:

*Mine eyes have seen the glory
of the coming of the Lord,
HASHEM is trampling out the vintage
where the grapes of wrath were stored.
HASHEM has loosed the fateful lightening
of that terrible swift sword
HASHEM's Truth is marching on.*

Glory, glory halleleuya(3X)

HASHEM's Truth is marching on.

**DRINKING THE SECOND
CUP OF WINE**

The second cup of wine is raised and all say:

We continue to sanctify this gathering with this second cup of wine.

בָּרוּךְ אַתָּה יְיָ אֱלֹהֵינוּ מֶלֶךְ הָעוֹלָם

Baruch ahta HASHEM, elohaynu melech haolam,

בּוֹרֵא פְּרִי הַגָּפֶן:

boray p'ree hagafen.

Blessed are you HASHEM, Nurturer of the Universe, for having given us the fruit of the vine, this second cup of Passover wine, the cup devoted to our ASKING for what we need. We have acknowledged the truth of the reality of the parts and aspects of our lives within which we want more choice, the IS-NESS of our lives. With this cup of wine we are ASKING for help with our growth.

As you drink the second cup of wine, feel it sliding down your throat, look inside in whatever way feels comfortable to you, and allow your inner voice to ask for the help that you need right now.

RACHTZAH:

hand washing before eating

רָחַץ

1   *All participants dip their fingertips into the water basin or symbolically rub their hands one against the other, and say:*

בָּרוּךְ אַתָּה יְיָ אֱלֹהֵינוּ מֶלֶךְ הָעוֹלָם

2   Baruch ahta HASHEM, Elohaynu melech ha-olam,

אֲשֶׁר קִדְּשָׁנוּ בְּמִצְוֹתָיו

asher kid'shonu bi-mitz-vo-tav,

וְצִוָּנוּ עַל-נְטִילַת יָדִים׃

vi-tzee-vanu oll ni-tee-lot yah-daiyim.

3   **Adored to us are you HASHEM, for reminding us again and again, of the holiness that is our fluid essence, and of our ability to be reminded of that essence and that holiness merely by touching our hands to each other and to water.**

MOE-TZEE MATZAH: מוֹצִיא

blessing over bread

1 *All gathered put their hands on the Matzah or on someone touching the Matzah and recite the following two prayers:*

בָּרוּךְ אַתָּה יְיָ אֱלֹהֵינוּ מֶלֶךְ הָעוֹלָם

2 Baruch ahta HASHEM, elohaynu melech haolam,

הַמּוֹצִיא לֶחֶם מִן-הָאָרֶץ:

ha-mo-tzee lechem min ha'aretz.

3 **Thank you HASHEM for creating a world wherein we can bring forth the component parts of bread, sustenance, from the earth.**

MATZAH: מַצָּה

a special blessing for matzah

בָּרוּךְ אַתָּה יְיָ אֱלֹהֵינוּ מֶלֶךְ הָעוֹלָם

4 Baruch ahta HASHEM, elohaynu melech haolam,

אֲשֶׁר קִדְּשָׁנוּ בְּמִצְוֹתָיו

asher kid-shah-nu bimitzvotav,

וְצִוָּנוּ עַל-אֲכִילַת מַצָּה:

vitzeevanu oll ah-chee-lot Matzah.

5 **Blessed are you HASHEM, Creator of the Universe, who has made us holy by giving us the Law, and within that Law obliged us to eat the special bread of Passover, the Matzah.**

Break off a piece of Matzah and eat it.

42

MAROR:

bitter herbs

בָּרוֹר

1 *A quantity of Maror, equivalent to an olive is eaten after the following prayer is said:*

בָּרוּךְ אַתָּה יְיָ אֱלֹהֵינוּ מֶלֶךְ הָעוֹלָם

2 Baruch ahta HASHEM, elohaynu melech haolam,

אֲשֶׁר קִדְּשָׁנוּ בְּמִצְוֹתָיו

asher kidshanu bimitzvotav,

וְצִוָּנוּ עַל־אֲכִילַת מָרוֹר

vitzeevanu oll acheelot mah-roar.

3 We recognize you HASHEM, we recognize your commandments and the ways in which we feel our holiness when we observe these command-ments, especially one as difficult as eating this Maror.

KORECH:

בּוֹרֵךְ

combination of matzah, maror and charoset

4 The charoset is a mixture of apples, nuts, wine and spices combined together to form a paste, symbolic of the mortar that our ancestors used to build the pyramids of Mitzrayim. But charoset is sweet; this is to remind us that in the midst of our slavery, our misery, there is always the potentiality of freedom, the sweet taste of freedom.

5 In remembrance of the Temple in Jerusalem, according to the custom of the great Sage, Hillel, we combine a piece of the third matzah with the maror and the charoset into a sandwich and eat it. Thus we intensify our remembrance of the slavery and the redemption.

SHULCHAN AHRUCH:

שֻׁלְחָן עוֹרֵךְ

eating the festive meal

6 We begin our meal with eating a hard-boiled egg dipped in salt water. Eggs have many meanings. They are the symbol of springtime, of death and its opposite, fertility, of the giving of life ... of new beginnings.

1 Most foods become softer, the longer they are in hot water; eggs, like Jews, become tougher. This is also true of the parts of ourselves that we try to hide, that we think we are setting aside; they too become tougher the more we let them boil.

2 *Take an egg of your own and all say together:*

We dip this egg in salt water to be reminded that there are tears that must accompany births and new beginnings; there are tears that accompany death and letting go. I honor the beginnings and the endings and the letting go

of living creatures in my life
whose presence hurt me,
of places that don't feel good for me;
of old behavior patterns that don't work for me;
of ways of earning my living that harm me;
of whatever it is that I need to let go of
to make room for a new beginning.

LET'S EAT!!!!

The reading of the Hagaddah is now halted and a full meal eaten. As the conclusion of the meal we eat the Afikoman, the dessert.

TZAFFON: צָפוּן

eating of the Afikoman

3

The Afikoman.
Lechem Oe-nee and Afikoman.
The bread of affliction
and the bread of the ultimate redemption.
After the pain, the pleasure.
After the pregnancy, the birth.
After the desert, the oasis.
After the tunnel, the Light.
After the exile, the homecoming;
After Mitzrayim, Eretz Yisroel.

4 **After the adults have redeemed the Afikoman from the child who found it, we eat a piece of it to symbolize our hope for the ultimate redemption of ourselves and all peoples, from affliction and oppression.**

The third cup of wine is filled.

BARECH

Recitation of thanks after the meal

בָּרֵךְ:

1   **We offer four blessings of thanks after we eat.**

2   **FIRST BLESSING: We give thanks to HASHEM for providing us with food.**

3   A story is told of Reb Zusha of Hanipoli.

Every day, after finishing his morning prayers, Reb Zusha would say: "Master of the universe, Zusha is hungry and wants to eat. Please furnish him with food." When his attendant would hear him speak these words he would serve him some cake and a drink.

One day, the attendant was cross and thought: "Why does the Rebbe ask HASHEM for food when I'm the one who always brings it to him?" He decided that on that day he would wait and not serve the Rebbe until he asked him directly.

4   Reb Zusha did not know of the attendant's feelings. In his usual way, he went for a morning mikveh (ritual immersion) and then dressed and was returning home. That day was a rainy day and the mud was thick. As he passed by a stranger to town, the stranger pushed him into the mud and walked off laughing, leaving Reb Zusha to pick himself up and make his way home.

The stranger proudly told the local innkeeper about the little Jew whom he had pushed into the mud. "What have you done, you fool," the innkeeper then said to him, "that was Reb Zusha you pushed into the mud!"

1 The stranger trembled in fear as Reb Zusha was known far and wide as a sacred mystic, as a holy man of God. "What shall I do?" he cried.

"Here," said the innkeeper, "take these sweets and this liquor to him after his prayers and beg his pardon. I'm sure that, righteous and modest as he is, he will most certainly forgive you."

Reb Zusha finished his prayers and said his words, "Master of the universe, Zusha is hungry and wishes to eat. Please furnish him with food."

His attendant heard him but didn't move. "If the Rebbe asks HASHEM for food, then let HASHEM bring it to him!"

Just then the door burst open and the stranger to town walked in carrying a tray of sweets and a drink. He went straight to Reb Zusha's study, put the tray of food before him and asked his forgiveness.

Thus did the attendant of Reb Zusha learn that it wasn't he who really provided the Rebbe with food, but rather it was, in truth, HASHEM.

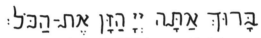

2 Baruch ahta HASHEM, ha-zaan et ha-kol.

3 **Blessed are you HASHEM, sustainer of all.**

4 **SECOND BLESSING: We give thanks to HASHEM for the earth and for providing us with food from the earth.**

5 Why does food have such a prominent place in the Passover Seder? What is so special about food on Pesach?

Grand Rabbi Levi Horowitz, The Bostonner Rebbe, teaches as follows:

Let us look to the Israelites journeying through the desert. They spent forty years learning about life, giving up the mental shackles of slavery to become a free people. In the desert HASHEM gave the Israelites three things in a miraculous fashion: the Torah, Manna (solid food), and spring water (liquid). Why these three things?

Could they not have had natural water instead of miraculous water? Is there a significance in the fact that it was Manna and spring water given with the Torah? The answer lies in the fact that they had to learn to appreciate that solid food and liquids are both part, and an important part, of a divine plan. They were given in a spiritual setting so that we would know that food must be respected for its spiritual quality.

1   This is not very obvious. We can say prayers and recognize the spirituality of the act; we can perform human deeds and there too, know we are committing a spiritual act. In eating, it is easy to think that one is performing a physical act of sustenance, pure and simple. Pesach helps us to see that this is not the case; it teaches us a basic concept of Judaism - the transformation of the physical to the spiritual.

In separating out for special notice the foods of Pesach, we are following the fact that this is the only holiday where food is prescribed. In addition, we are celebrating our freedom and unity as a people. And finally, we are recognizing and rejoicing at the spirituality that is inherent and woven through all facets of our lives.

בָּרוּךְ אַתָּה יִי עַל הָאָרֶץ וְעַל הַמָּזוֹן:

2   Baruch ahta HASHEM, ol ha-aretz vi-ol ha-mazon.

3   **Thank you HASHEM, for the earth and the food.**

4   **THIRD BLESSING: We give thanks to HASHEM for the holy city of Jerusalem and for our tribal homeland, Israel.**

5
How can we sing the songs of God
when we live on earth that is foreign soil?
If I forget thee O Jerusalem,
you should cause me to forget my power.
My tongue should be silenced
if I don't remember you,
if I don't go up to Jerusalem
at the peak of my joy.

(Psalms 137)

1   We give thanks for this lesson of the importance of "place," the importance of having a tribal homeland, a spiritual center. We give thanks for the reality of that which a Jewish homeland allows us: the ability to practice Judaism openly.

We give thanks for the sacred spark in our souls that is the image of Jerusalem - her air, her hills, the sound of prayer, the stones of The Wall, the vision of the faces of all the world's people, the peace of Shabbat.

2   We pray for peace between the cousins: between the children of Abraham, Isaac and Jacob and the children of Esau and Ishmael.

3   We pray for peace in Jerusalem and in all other places that have more than one tribe who consider it their tribal homeland.

בָּרוּךְ אַתָּה יְיָ בּוֹנֶה בְּרַחֲמָיו יְרוּשָׁלַיִם אָמֵן׃

4   Baruch ahta HASHEM, boe-nay bi-rachamav Yerushalayim, amen.

5   **Thank you HASHEM for the moments of mercy when you build and rebuild both the geographic Jerusalem as well as the Jerusalems of the spirit, the sacred spaces.**

48

1   **FOURTH BLESSING: We give thanks for loving-kindness wherever it manifests.**

2   A father once complained to the Baal Shem-Tov that his son had forsaken God. "What should I do?" he cried to the Besht.

  "Love him more than ever," the Baal Shem-Tov replied.

3   Blessed are you HASHEM - Creator, Designer, Definer - who feeds the whole world: who provides physical sustenance for the body and compassion and mercy for the soul. Nurturer of all living creatures; teacher of the lessons of unconditional love and eternal chesed, loving-kindness. Thank you for sharing with us the gift of universal generosity and goodness. When we integrate this lesson into our souls we are able to be happy with our portion, we never feel a sense of "lack."

בָּרוּךְ אַתָּה יְיָ הַטּוֹב וְהַמֵּיטִיב לַכֹּל:

4   Baruch ahta HASHEM, ha-tov vi-ha-may-teev la-kol.

5   **Thank you HASHEM, for bringing to us the light of goodness, thus making us better human beings.**

6   **THE PROPHET ELIYAHU**

In the second book of Kings, (Melachim Bet), the Prophet

Eliyahu (Elijah) is last seen ascending to heaven in a fiery chariot pulled by fiery horses. A tradition grew up around Eliyahu, that he would return to prophesize the arrival of the Messiah.

1   But his return, and the dawn of this Messianic Age, a truly New Age, are thought to be dependent on people's actions: on the way we treat ourselves, each other, all living creatures and the earth; on our observance of the commandments. For it is only when people have reached a high level of humanity, when they practice loving-kindness in all facets of their lives, that the possibility of a Messianic Era can become a reality.

2   In acknowledgement of the role we each play in making possible a new Messianic Era, we look to our own actions and to the actions of others; we look for these actions of Chesed, of loving-kindness. To each of one of these actions we say, "Amen, may it continue to be so."

3   *Place a special empty wine-cup for the Prophet Elijah in a central place on the Passover table. As each of the following ten groups of individuals is acknowledged, whoever is moved to do so, should spill some wine from their third cup of Passover wine into the special cup, till the cup is almost, but not completely, full. If you want to, you can continue to call out groups of people or individuals who should be recognized for their actions; actions that you believe help to bring on a Messianic Era, a New Age.*

MAY IT CONTINUE TO BE SO:

4   To those who follow the example of our first forefather, Abraham, and show love, generosity and welcome, to the lost, the lonely, the sick, the poor, and even to the parts of themselves they don't like, we say:

All speak: Amen, may it continue to be so.

1   To those who treat all living creatures, starting with themselves and including planet earth, with respect and caring, we say:

All speak: Amen, may it continue to be so.

2   To those who give charity, who help others to find work, who help others to find mates, we say:

All speak: Amen, may it continue to be so.

3   To those who speak out for justice even when all around them there is just silence, we say:

All speak: Amen, may it continue to be so.

4   To those who work to strengthen and build community, we say:

All speak: Amen, may it continue to be so.

5   To those who follow the example of our first foremother, Sarah, and practice the lesson of boundaries: remembering that "yes" has no meaning if you cannot say "no," - and then say "yes" and "no" as appropriate, we say:

All speak: Amen, may it continue to be so.

6   To those who own 'responsibility,' who seek to understand their own Chometz and their own "Mitzrayim," the way they participate in limiting themselves, rather than always seeking to ascribe blame; to those who create the context they need from within which they can make personal changes, we say:

All speak: Amen, may it continue to be so.

1   To those who seek to create understanding, to make peace, to put an end to revenge-wars and killings, we say:

All speak: Amen, may it continue to be so.

2   To those who realize that life is short and universally precious, we say:

All speak: Amen, may it continue to be so.

3   To those who want to learn about and/or recreate Jewish rituals, starting with Shabbat - a day of BEING rather than DOING, one day a week of a reality created by inward search, outward prayer, in-person communications, learning and making love - and then do their best to observe, we say:

All speak: Amen, may it continue to be so.

4   In the final analysis WE MUST ASK:

Am I taking actions to help myself? to help others?

5   Am I living as an enslaved person believing and acting as if there is no possibility for change or am I searching for what I can do to create a context for change?

6   Am I doing everything that I can to help to heal the planet and her inhabitants?

7   If I were to be twenty years older than I am today, looking back at this time, would there be things that I would regret that I had not done, could no longer do or would no longer make a difference even if I did them?

8   Have I sought to learn, or relearn, or reinterpret any aspect of my heritage?

**1   DRINKING THE THIRD
CUP OF WINE**

*Everyone lifts up their cups of
wine and says:*

We continue to sanctify this gathering with this third cup of wine.

2

בָּרוּךְ אַתָּה יְיָ אֱלֹהֵינוּ מֶלֶךְ הָעוֹלָם,

Baruch ahta HASHEM, elohaynu, melech ha-o-lam, bo-ray

בּוֹרֵא פְּרִי הַגָּפֶן:

3   **We are thankful to you HASHEM, active force in the universe, for having
created the fruit of the vine, this third cup of Passover wine, the cup of
ACTION, the cup of DOING. We thank you for the vibration of energy,
the movement of light that has resulted in the creation of the world. We
thank you for this lesson, the corollary of the lesson of the second cup
of wine, that in addition to ASKING, we have to do work, to TAKE
ACTION, to perform deeds, to create an appropriate context within
which a desirable outcome is possible.**

4   *Drink most of the third cup of wine; leave over a few drops. Then open the door for Eliyahu.*

5   **SHEFACH CHAHMAT-CHAH:**   **And there are individuals walking
the planet today who have awareness that their actions cause harm in
the present and to the future and even so, they persist with these
actions. It is for them that the concept of** shefach chahmatchah, **of asking
that 'rage and wrath should be unleashed,' is spoken.**

6   We are reminded of the story of the old man who was planting a carob tree.
"Why do you plant a tree that will not bear fruit for seventy years?" he was
asked. "Do you expect to live to eat the fruit of your labor?"

"No," the old man responded, "but I did not find the world a barren place
when I was born into it. As my fathers planted for me before I was born, so
do I plant for the children who will come after me."

Mishnah Ta'anit 23a

1   **We ask that those who with their actions plant the seeds of misery or the seeds of hypocrisy or the seeds of pollution or the seeds of destruction be allowed to see, feel and taste of the fruit of these actions:**

2   Those who instigate wars, who force children out to kill or be killed, to learn a lesson of "it's them or us".

3   Those who participate in creating untrue reality maps when they lie by commission or by omission.

4   Those who use their religious or political belief systems to create distance and disharmony between themselves and their fellow travelers on planet earth.

5   Those who trick, cheat or steal from those more helpless than themselves -- the elderly, the widow, the immigrant, the employee.

6   Those who physically, emotionally or sexually abuse their spouses, children, parents, or animals and then don't even seek psychological help.

7   Those who first, last and always only think of themselves, who behave thoughtlessly and dishonor the concept of "friendship."

8   Those who are unwilling to take responsibility; those who are quick to blame others without seeking to understand the part they play(ed) in a given outcome.

9   Those who self-righteously condemn other countries for doing what they or their country did at another time in history.... Those who ask other people and other nations to do what they themselves are unwilling to do.

1   Those who put profit before life -- those who burn grain rather than give it away; those who cut down the rain forests; those who use animals for cosmetics testing; those who create internal and external pollution: those who make the decisions to allow toxic gases to be emitted in the workplace and hazardous waste to be disposed of in an unacceptable fashion.

2   Those who are unwilling to change their lifestyle to ensure the survival of the planet.

3   (Are there any others whose deeds need to be mentioned here?)

4   **And if after tasting the fruit of their actions, they still choose to continue with these actions, then onto them we say:** SHEHFACH CHAH-MATCHAH, **may an appropriate form of** chahmah, **of wrath, be spilled upon them.**

שְׁפֹךְ חֲמָתְךָ

5   **COMMITMENT TO ACTION:**   The Kotzker Rebbe used to say: 'There are three ways in which a person can go about performing a good deed. A person can say, 'I will do the deed soon.' This is a poor way. They can say: 'I am ready to do it now.' This is better. But the person who says, 'I am doing it now,' that person is praiseworthy.

6   *All speak:* I have read the list of deeds that support the coming of a Messianic Era; I have looked into my soul and I acknowledge those supportive deeds that I undertake as part of my daily existence. I have read the list of negative actions and I know which ones, if any, I am guilty of committing. Now it is time for me to face these people with whom I share this Passover Seder and to publically, verbally commit myself to at least one deed I will undertake in the coming year, that will help me to get myself out of my own self-generated Mitzrayim and to at least one action that will help to heal the planet.

7   *In groups of eight or smaller, share your commitments to deeds and to actions for this year. Speak them in the first person and as if you are already doing them. Then add the leftover drops of wine from your third cup of wine to Eliyahu's cup of wine, thus filling it with wine from our own cups, related to the commitments we make.*

1 **Thus will we bring the Prophet Eliyahu:**

The Chant For Eliyahu
(3 times)

2 E-li-ya-hu Ha-na-vi   אֵלִיָּהוּ הַנָּבִיא   **Eliyahu, the prophet**

E-li-ya-hu Ha-teesh-be   אֵלִיָּהוּ הַתִּשְׁבִּי   **Eliyahu, from Tishbi**

Eliyahu, Eliyahu   אֵלִיָּהוּ אֵלִיָּהוּ   **Eliyahu, Eliyahu**

Eliyahu Ha-geel-a-di   אֵלִיָּהוּ הַגִּלְעָדִי   **Eliyahu, from Gilad.**

Beem-hay-ra Bi-ya-maynu   בִּמְהֵרָה בְיָמֵינוּ   **In a hurry, in our lifetime**

Yah-voe ay-laynu   יָבוֹא אֵלֵינוּ   **Let him come to us.**

Eem moe-she-ach ben David   עִם מָשִׁיחַ בֶּן דָּוִד   **With the Messiah, from the House of David.**

Eem moe-she-ach ben David   עִם מָשִׁיחַ בֶּן דָּוִד   **With the Messiah, from the House of David.**

1

Fill a fourth cup of Passover wine.

HALLEL

give praise and let it shine

הַלֵּל

2 **Leader: This second half of the Hallel is made up of meditations, chants and readings of praise and thanksgiving to HASHEM.** I invite everyone to sit back, relax and allow their mind's eye to visualize what it will, while I slowly read the following Hallel meditation.

3

A Hallel Meditation:

At the first, in the beginning, there was just the Beingness,
the Darkness, the Oneness
the Aine Sof,
HASHEM.

From this Oneness,
in the midst of the Darkness,
was the 'toe-who va-voe-who:'
the confusion,
the inability to tell the difference
between where the sky ended
and the waters began.

And after the darkness
and after the confusion,
HASHEM:
the Great Mystery of Oneness,
the Beingness we cannot comprehend,
the face we cannot know;
HASHEM:
created solidity of 'Form.'
And the form that was created was Earth.

Form.
Earth.
Mother Earth.
Creation of Life Form:
Vegetation Life Form,
Sea Life Form,
Wing-ed Life Form,
Four-leggeds, Two-leggeds.
But Life form without Life Force,
Without The Breath.

From HASHEM came The Breath;
through HASHEM moved The Life Force
into the Life-forms:
breathing for them
breathing with them
giving them The Breath.
Thus came light and life to our planet.

Honor the great mystery of HASHEM.
Honor the creations.
WE are the creations:
multiple facets of the unknowable,
the whole we call 'HASHEM'.
Complementary parts/opposing parts,
for goodness and for evil:
open and closed,
spiritually
intellectually,
emotionally,
physically.
Innumerable images,
innumerable parts,
all needing acceptance,
all needing acknowledgment,
of the truth
of right now.

Tonight we honor HASHEM,
the One,
the great mystery,
the primal knowingness,
HASHEM.

We honor the dry earth
and the wet seas,
the air and the heavens.
We honor the four-leggeds,
the crawlers,
the flyers,
the swimmers.

We honor the multi-faceted
grand-finale creation:
Humanity.

WE HONOR THE INTERCONNECTEDNESS OF ALL.

There are moments when we forget who we are: we forget our power, we forget our joy. And at those times:

מִן הַמֵּצַר קָרָאתִי יָהּ׃

Min ha-may-tzar kah-rah-tee: YAH!

עֲנָנִי בַמֶּרְחַבְיָהּ׃

Ah-nah-nee bah-merchav YAH.

**From the narrowing confines
of my distress,
I call out,
"YAH!"**

**And YAH then opens
up a space in me
so that I can remember
who I am,
I can remember
my self-confidence.**

**I can remember that HASHEM,
in the personification of YAH,
of loving-kindness,
provides my direction.
I can remember that I do not have to fear
and just follow the direction of man.**

**I can remember that HASHEM will support me
in my chosen direction through the helpers
who come to me.
HASHEM will even allow me to see into the souls
of those who hate me,
those who try to divert me from my path.**

**It is advisable to seek refuge in HASHEM
rather than to have trusting expectations of people.
It is advisable to seek refuge in HASHEM,
rather than to have trusting expectations
of those who urge you on
from positions of earth-based power.**

Min ha-may-tzar kah-rah-tee YAH!
Ah-nah-nee bah-merchav YAH.

אוֹדְךָ כִּי עֲנִיתָנִי וַתְּהִי לִי לִישׁוּעָה׃

1 Oh-dih-chah key ah-nee-tah-nee va-ti-he lee le-yi-shuah.

2 **I will give thanks and I will praise you because you bring answers to me
and thus, are my salvation.**

אֶבֶן מָאֲסוּ הַבּוֹנִים הָיְתָה לְרֹאשׁ פִּנָּה׃

3 Eh-ven ma-ah-su ha-boenim, ha-yitah li-rosh pee-nah.

4 **I am like the stone that is first rejected by the
builders
and then is chosen to be the cornerstone.**

5 May-ate HASHEM ha-yitah zut, he nif-layt bi-aye-nay-nu.

6 **This possibility comes only from HASHEM,
and is an awesome wonder in our eyes.**

זֶה הַיּוֹם עָשָׂה יְיָ נָגִילָה וְנִשְׂמְחָה בוֹ׃

7 Zeh ha-yum ah-sah HASHEM, nah-gee-lah vi-nis-micha bo.

8 **And so this is the day that HASHEM has created for us
to be happy
and to make sounds
of ecstatic joy.**

60

Song: Hava Nageela

1 הָבָה נָגִילָה וְנִשְׂמְחָה

Hava Nageela(3X)
Vi-nis-mi-chah
(2X)

2 הָבָה נְרַנְּנָה וְנִשְׂמְחָה

Hava Ni-rah-nih-na (3X)
Vi-nis-mi-chah
(2X)

3 עוּרוּ, עוּרוּ אַחִים

Ooh-roo, ooh-roo ah-chim

עוּרוּ אַחִים בְּלֵב
שָׂמֵחַ

4 Ooh-roo achim bi-layv sah-may-ach (5X)
(alternate 'achim' with 'achut')

5 Come let us be glad and rejoice,
Come let us sing and be gay.
Awake my brothers and my sisters
with a joyful heart.

6 *Leader:* אָנָּא יְיָ הוֹשִׁיעָה נָא:

Ah-nah HASHEM, hoe-she-ah nah.

7 *All say:* **Answer me HASHEM, and save me.**

8 *Leader:* אָנָּא יְיָ הַצְלִיחָה נָא:

Ah-nah HASHEM, hah-tzlee-chah nah.

9 *All say:* **Answer me HASHEM,
and help me to succeed.**

1   Rabbi Hillel: "If I am not for myself, who will be for me?.... But if I am only for myself, what am I? .... And if not now, when?"

2   *Song: This Little Light of Mine*

This little light of mine,
I'm going to let it shine! (3X)

Let it shine, let it shine, let it shine.

(Fill in words that have meaning to you,
for example:
(1) When I'm feeling down and out -
I'm going to let it shine!

(2) When I'm feeling really good -
I'm going to let it shine!

(3) When I'm feeling all alone -
I'm going to let it shine!

(4) When I'm looking for liberation-
I'm going to let it shine!)

3   **PREPARATION FOR DRINKING THE FOURTH CUP OF WINE** The fourth cup of wine, the final cup of Passover wine, is the cup of TRUST, of letting go and trusting, fully and completely, in HASHEM, in the One. We have done an intense internal examination and we know the truth of our current reality. From within the context of self-knowledge, we have asked for whatever it is that we need or want. We have searched and seen what we are already doing; we have committed to do additional things so as to create the context within which change, evolution and healing can occur. Now it is the time to let go and trust -- to open ourselves up to the vulnerability within which movement can happen.

4   And trusting is difficult; things often don't seem to work out as we expected, as we would have wanted. We may feel hurt, we may feel abandoned, we may feel angry: "Again I trusted and again I was disappointed," we say. "Why has God abandoned me now when I am most in need of support?" we ask.

1   Two folk tales on Trust and on being Supported:

2   There was a man who walked through life with the belief that HASHEM walked by his side. When he would look down at the footprints created in the dirt he walked on, he would see two sets of footprints. A time came, when he had to cross a desert - a long and very treacherous desert. He began to despair of ever getting to the other side: his energy was running out, his will was walking away from him, his trust was totally gone. And when he looked down to see the footprints in the sand, he saw only one set.

     "How can you leave me now when I most need you!" he screamed at HASHEM. "How can you abandon me now!"

3   "I haven't abandoned you," he heard in reply. "I am still with you. If you see only one set of footprints it is because I hear your pain, I recognize your anguish and so I have taken you into my arms and I am carrying you. The footprints you see in the sand are mine!"

4   And then there was Shloimie the farmer in the shtetl in Eastern Europe. Shloimie was a poor farmer; he had a son, a cow, and a small field. One day his cow ran off and was gone.

     "Oy, poor Shloimie," the shtetl people said. "What will become of him now that his cow has run off?"

     Three days later his cow returned and with it were four other wild cows and a bull. "Oh, how lucky Shloimie is," said the shtetl people, "now Shloimie will have so much milk he will be able to sell some."

     The next day Shloimie's son broke his leg. "Oy, poor Shloimie! Such terrible news; his one son, his one helper, has broken his leg and can't do anything! So terrible."

1   Three days later, the Tzar called up all the young boys to be in his army. "Oh, how lucky Shloimie is," said the shtetl people, "Shloimie is the one man in the shtetl whose son does not have to go into the Tzar's army because he has a broken leg!"

2   So there are times when what seems like a bad situation, ends up as a good situation and vice versa. We don't know what will be tommorrow; the novel that is our lives just moves from chapter to chapter, each chapter building on the one before it. And there are those who believe that even death is not the final chapter, because the neshamah, the soul, lives on and chooses it's next life based on what it has to learn, on how far it has come in this lifetime.

3   **DRINKING THE FOURTH CUP OF PASSOVER WINE**

    We will end the ritual part of this Pass- over Seder by drinking the fourth cup of wine, and saying a prayer of completion.

4   **We continue to sanctify this gathering with this fourth cup of Passover wine.**

בָּרוּךְ אַתָּה יְיָ אֱלֹהֵינוּ מֶלֶךְ הָעוֹלָם

5   Baruch ahta HASHEM, Eloheynu melech ha-o-lam,

בּוֹרֵא פְּרִי הַגָּפֶן:

bo-ray pree ha-ga-fen.

6   **We are thankful to you, HASHEM, Healer of the Universe, for having created the fruit of the vine this fourth cup of Passover wine, the cup of LETTING GO and TRUSTING.**

7   **We recognize how hard it is to maintain the internal vibration of trust, of believing that all is as it should be and that we must let go and let HASHEM take over. We know that we have done all that we can.**

8   **We thank you HASHEM for all your creations, living messages of our faith: for the vine and the fruit of the vine; for the land you have given us as an inheritance; for Jerusalem; for this Passover feast. As we drink this wine, we let go and trust.**

9   *Drink the fourth cup of Passover wine.*

NIRTZAH

גֵּרְצָה

request for acceptance of prayers

1 *All speak:* **We have completed this Passover Seder and fulfilled our obligations according to law and custom. We ask that You accept our prayers, that You lead us out of the Mitzrayims of the soul in which we find ourselves and into the Jerusalem of the soul - a place of beauty, abundance, openness and grace.**

2 *A large bowl should be set in the middle of the Seder table. Any participant in the Seder who has not yet made a list of their chometz, i.e. the actions they take and the beliefs they carry that hold them back from being the best person they can be, must now do so. When they are done, all participants should take a few minutes to look at their lists and make yet another list. Included in this new list should be all those items – beliefs and actions - that they are willing to let go of right now.*

Each person, in turn, should take their list, shred it, stop for a few seconds and then throw it in the bowl. After everyone has thrown their shredded lists into the bowl, if the bowl is fireproof, then the leader can set it afire. If it is not fireproof, then the shreds can be thrown into a fireplace to be burned or they can be disposed of in some other way that seems appropriate to all in attendance.

NEXT   YEAR   IN   JERUSALEM!

THE TABLE SONGS

At the conclusion of the traditional Passover Seder are the medieval table songs. Though simple and playful, often thought to be included to reawaken the interest of the children, their underlying motives are religious in nature.

AH-DEER WHO:

a song praising HASHEM with every letter of the alphabet

1   Ah-deer who (2X)

Glorious is HASHEM!   אַדִּיר הוּא

Chorus:

2   Yiv-neh bay-toe bih-kah-ruv.   יִבְנֶה בֵּיתוֹ בְּקָרוֹב
**May the House of HASHEM,
those who follow the ways of HASHEM,
be rebuilt and built up soon.**

בִּמְהֵרָה בִּמְהֵרָה בְּיָמֵינוּ בְּקָרוֹב ׃
Bim-hay-ra-a-ah, bim-hay-rah, bi-yah-may-nu bih-kah-rov.
In a hurry, in our lifetime, soon.

אֵל בְּנֵה, אֵל בְּנֵה, בְּנֵה בֵּיתוֹ בְּקָרוֹב ׃
El binay, el binay, binay bay-toe bih-kah-ah-rov.
HASHEM rebuild Your house through coming near to us.

3   Bah-chur who   **Elected is HASHEM**   בָּחוּר הוּא

4   Gah-dul who   **Great is HASHEM**   גָּדוֹל הוּא

5   Dah-gul who   **Distinguished is HASHEM**   דָּגוּל הוּא

Chorus:

6   Hah-dur who   **The highest manifestation of power is HASHEM**   הָדוּר הוּא

7   Vah-teek who   **Faithful is HASHEM**   וָתִיק הוּא

66

#			
1	Zah-kai who	**Faultless is HASHEM**	זַכַּאי הוּא
2	Chassid who	**Lovingly kind is HASHEM**	חָסִיד הוּא
		Chorus	
3	Tah-hore who	**Pure is HASHEM**	טָהוֹר הוּא
4	Yah-cheed who	**Unique is HASHEM**	יָחִיד הוּא
5	Kah-beer who	**Strong is HASHEM**	כַּבִּיר הוּא
6	Lah-muud who	**All-wise is HASHEM**	לָמוּד הוּא
7	Meh-lech who	**Ruler is HASHEM**	מֶלֶךְ הוּא
8	Noh-rah who	**Awesome is HASHEM**	נוֹרָא הוּא
9	Sah-geev who	**Sublime is HASHEM**	שַׂגִּיב הוּא
10	Eey-zuuz who	**A Refuge is HASHEM**	עִזּוּז הוּא
11	Poe-deh who	**Redeemer is HASHEM**	פּוֹדֶה הוּא
12	Tzaddik who	**All-righteous is HASHEM**	צַדִּיק הוּא
		Chorus	
13	Kah-doshe who	**Holy is HASHEM**	קָדוֹשׁ הוּא
14	Rah-choom who	**Compassionate is HASHEM**	רַחוּם הוּא

1 Shah-dai who   **Almighty is HASHEM**   שַׁדַּי הוּא

2 Tah-keef who   **Omnipotent is HASHEM**   תַּקִּיף הוּא

Chorus

EH-CHAD ME YOE-DAI-YA
a song of our precious gifts

3 Echod me yoe-dai-ya?   **Who knows One?**   אֶחָד מִי יוֹדֵעַ?

4 Echod ah-nee yoe-dai-ya.   **I know One.**

5 * Echod eh-lo-hay-nu sheh-ba-sha-mai-yim ooh-vah-aretz.
One is HASHEM in heaven and on earth.

6 Shnai-yim me yoe-dai-ya?   **Who knows two?**   שְׁנַיִם מִי יוֹדֵעַ?

7 Shnai-yim ah-nee yoe-dah-aht.   **I know two.**

8 * Shnaie loo-chut ha-breet, echod eh-lo-hay-nu sheh-ba-sha-mai-yim ooh-vah-aretz.
Two are the tablets of the covenant.

9 Shlow-shah me yoe-dai-yah?   **Who knows three?**   שְׁלֹשָׁה מִי יוֹדֵעַ?

10 Shlow-shah ah-nee yoe-dai-ya.   **I know three.**

11 * Shlow-shah ah-vut, shnaie loo-chut ha-breet, echod eh-lo-hay-nu sheh-ba-sha-mai-yim ooh-vah-aretz.
Three are the Fathers of Israel.

1 Ahr-bah me yoe-dai-yah? **אַרְבַּע מִי יוֹדֵעַ?**
   Who knows four?

2 Ahr-bah ah-nee yoe-dah-aht.
   I know four

3 * Ahr-bah eeh-mah-hut, shlow-shah ah-vut, shnai loo-chut ha-breet, echod eh-lo-hay-nu sheh-ba-sha-mai-yim ooh-vah-aretz.
   Four are the mothers of Israel.

4 Chah-me-shah me yoe-dai-yah? **חֲמִשָׁה מִי יוֹדֵעַ?**
   Who knows five?

5 Chah-me-shah ah-nee yoe-dai-ya.
   I know five.

6 * Chah-me-shah choom-shay Torah, ahr-bah eeh-mah-hut, shlow-shah ah-vut, shnai loo-chut ha-breet, echod eh-lo-hay-nu sheh-ba-sha-mai-yim ooh-vah-aretz.
   Five are the books of the Torah.

7 She-shah me yoe-dai-yah? **שִׁשָׁה מִי יוֹדֵעַ?**
   Who knows six?

8 She-shah ah-nee yoe-dah-at.
   I know six.

9 * She-shah see-dray mishnah, chah-me-shah choom-shay Torah, ahr-bah eeh-mah-hut, shlow-shah ah-vut, shnai loo-chut ha-breet, echod eh-lo-hay-nu sheh-ba-sha-mai-yim ooh-vah-aretz.
   Six are the books of the Mishnah.

10 Sheev-ah me yoe-dai-yah? **שִׁבְעָה מִי יוֹדֵעַ?**
    Who knows seven?

11 Sheev-ah ah-nee yoe-dai-yah.
    I know seven.

12 * Sheev-ah yi-may sha-bah-ta, she-shah see-dray mishnah, chah-me-shah choom-shay Torah, ahr-bah eeh-mah-hut, shlow-shah ah-vut, shnai loo-chut ha-breet, echod eh-lo-hay-nu sheh-ba-sha-mai-yim ooh-vah-aretz.
    Seven are the days of the week.

1. Shmoe-nah me yoe-dai-yah?
Who knows eight?

עְמוֹנָה מִי יוֹדֵעַ?

2. Shmoe-nah ah-nee yoe-dah-at.
I know eight.

3. * Shmoe-nah yih-may mee-lah, sheev-ah yi-may sha-bah-ta, she-shah see-dray mishnah, chah-me-shah choom-shay Torah, ahr-bah eeh-ma-hut, shlow-shah ah-vut, shnai loo-chut ha-breet, echod eh-lo-hay-nu sheh-ba-sha-mai-yim ooh-vah-aretz.
Eight are the days till circumcision.

4. Tee-shah me yoe-dai-yah?
Who knows nine?

5. Tee-shah ah-nee yoe-dai-yah.
I know nine.

6. * Tee-shah yahr-chay lay-dah, shmoe-nah yih-may mee-lah, sheev-ah yi-may sha-bah-ta, she-shah see-dray mishnah, chah-me-shah choom-shay Torah, ahr-bah eeh-ma-hut, shlow-shah ah-vut, shnai loo-chut ha-breet, echod eh-lo-hay-nu sheh-ba-sha-mai-yim ooh-vah-aretz.
Nine are the months of pregnancy.

7. Ah-sah-rah me yoe-dai-yah?
Who knows ten?

עֲשָׂרָה מִי יוֹדֵעַ?

8. Ah-sah-rah ah-nee yoe-dah-aht.
I know ten.

9. * Ah-sah-rah dee-brah-yah, tee-shah yahr-chay lay-dah, shmoe-nah yih-may mee-lah, sheev-ah yi-may sha-bah-ta, she-shah see-dray mishnah, chah-me-shah choom-shay Torah, ahr-bah eeh-ma-hut, shlow-shah ah-vut, shnai loo-chut ha-breet, echod eh-lo-hay-nu sheh-ba-sha-mai-yim ooh-vah-aretz.
Ten are the Divine Commandments.

אַחַד עָשָׂר מִי יוֹדֵעַ?

10. Ah-chad ah-sar me yoe-dai-yah?
Who knows eleven?

11. Ah-chad ah-sar ah-nee yoe-dai-yah.
I know eleven.

12. * Ah-chad ah-sar kuch-vah-yah, ah-sah-rah dee-brah-yah, tee-shah yahr-chay lay-dah, shmoe-nah yih-may mee-lah, sheev-ah yimay shahbahta, sheeshah see-dray mishnah, chahmeshah choomshay Torah, ahrbah eeymahut, shlowshah

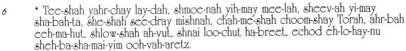

ahvut, shnai loochut habreet, echod chlohaynu shehbashamaiyim oohvaharetz.
Eleven are the stars that bowed to Joseph.

1 Shnaym ah-sar me yoe-dai-yah? שְׁנֵים עָשָׂר מִי יוֹדֵעַ?
Who knows twelve?

2 Shnaym ah-sar ah-nee yoe-dah-aht.
I know twelve.

3 * Shnaym ah-sar shiv-tah-yah, ah-chad ah-sar kuchvahyah, ahsahrah, deebrahyah, teeshah yahrchay laydah, shmoenah yihmay meelah, sheevah yimay shahbahta, sheeshah seedray mishnah, chahmeshah choomshay Torah, ahrbah eeymahut, shlowshah ahvut, shnai loochut habreet, echod chlohaynu shehbashamaiyim oohvaharetz.
Twelve are the Tribes of Israel.

4 Shlowsh ah-sar me yoe-dai-yah? שְׁלֹשָׁה עָשָׂר מִי יוֹדֵעַ?
Who knows thirteen?

5 Shlowsh ah-sar ah-nee yoe-dai-yah.
I know thirteen.

6 * Shlowsh ah-sar mee-dah-yah, shnaym ahsar shivtahyah, ahchad ahsar kuchvahyah, ahsahrah deebrahyah, teeshah yahrchay laydah, shmoenah yihmay meelah, sheevah yimay shahbahta, sheeshah seedray mishnah, chahmeshah choomshay Torah, ahrbah eeymahut, shlowshah ahvut, shnai loochut habreet, echod chlohaynu shehbashamaiyim oohvaharetz.
Thirteen are the attributes of HASHEM.

CHAD GADYA

a symbolic song of our history

7 Chad gadya, chad gadya. חַד גַּדְיָא. חַד גַּדְיָא.
One kid, one kid.

8 Di-zah-been ahbah be-tray zoozay. *Chorus:* דְּזַבִּין אַבָּא בִּתְרֵי זוּזֵי.
That father bought for two zuzim.

Chad gadya, chad gadya. חַד גַּדְיָא חַד גַּדְיָא:
One kid, one kid.
(The Ten Commandments engraved on two tablets of stone).

1   Vi-ahta shoon-rah vi-ahchlah li-gadya. *Chorus.*
A cat came and devoured the kid.
(Babylon destroyed Jerusalem and the Temple).

Vi-ahta chal-bah vi-nah-shach li-shoon-rah. Di-ahch-lah li-gadya. *Chorus.*
A dog came and bit the cat.
(Persia overthrew Babylon).

2   Vi-ahta choot-ra vi-hee-kah li-chal-bah. Di-nah-shach li-shoon-rah. Di-ahch-lah li-gadya. *Chorus.*
A stick came and beat the dog.
(Greece vanquished Persia).

וְאָתָא נוּרָא וְשָׂרַף לְחוּטְרָא...

3   Vi-ahta noo-rah vi-sah-rahf li-choot-rah. Di-hee-kah li-chal-bah. Di-nah-shach li-shoon-rah. Di-ahch-lah li-gadya. *Chorus.*
A fire came and burnt the stick.
(Rome conquered Greece).

וְאָתָא מַיָּא וּכְבָה לְנוּרָא...

4   Vi-ahta mai-yah vi-chah-vah li-noo-rah. Di-sah-rahf li-choot-rah. Di-hee-kah li-chal-bah. Di-nah-shach li-shoonrah. Di-ahch-lah li-gadya. *Chorus.*
Water came and quenched the fire.
(Barbarian invaders overwhelmed Rome).

וְאָתָא תוֹרָא וְשָׁתָה לְמַיָּא...

5   Vi-ahta toe-rah vi-shah-tah li-mai-yah. Di-chah-vah li-noo-rah. Di-sah-rahf li-choot-rah. Di-hee-kah li-chal-bah. Di-nah-shach li-shoon-rah. Di-ahch-lah li-gadya. *Chorus.*
An ox came and drank the water.
(Moslem powers came and absorbed all).

1   Vi-ahta hah-show-chet, vi-shah-chaat li-toe-rah. Di-shah-tah li-mai-yah. Di-chah-vah li-noo-rah. Di-sah-rahf li-choot-rah. Di-hee-kah li-chal-bah. Di-nah-shach li-shoon-rah. Di-ahch-lah li-gadya.
Chorus.

The slaughterer came and slaughtered the ox.
(Crusaders overthrew the Moslems).

וְאָתָא מַלְאַךְ הַמָּוֶת וְשָׁחַט לְשׁוֹחֵט

2   Vi-ahta mah-laach ha-maavet vi-shah-chaat li-show-chet. Di-shah-chaat li-toe-rah. Di-shah-tah li-mai-yah. Di-chah-vah li-noo-rah. Di-sah-rahf li-choot-rah. Di-hee-kah li-chal-bah. Di-nah-shach li-shoon-rah. Di-ahch-lah li-gadya. *Chorus.*

The angel of death killed the slaughterer.
(The reign of violence will be ended through heavenly intervention)

וְאָתָא הַקָּדוֹשׁ בָּרוּךְ הוּא וְשָׁחַט לְמַלְאַךְ הַמָּוֶת...

3   Vi-ahta Ha-kahdush Ba-ruch Who vi-shah-chaat li-mah-laach ha-maavet. Di-shah-chaat li-show-chet. Di-shah-chaat li-toe-rah. Di-shah-tah li-mai-yah. Di-chah-vah li-noo-rah. Di-sah-rahf li-choot-rah. Di-hee-kah li-chal-bah. Di-nah-shach li-shoon-rah. Di-ahch-lah li-gadya. *Chorus.*

And the Holy One, HASHEM, came and slew the angel of death.
(In the end, HASHEM will establish a New Age of Chassidut).

4   **CLOSING PRAYERS:**   In closing, we say a prayer for the path, a Tefillat Ha'Derech, because in truth, we are all creating our own individual paths, hopefully paths leading to greater personal and planetary healing, with each step we take. Sometimes we cross paths, as we have tonight - we come closer and we break apart, closer and apart, a part of and apart from. And when our paths take us far apart, as they will once again in the not-too-far-distant future, it is nice, it will be nice, to have the prayers and the blessings of those with whom we have broken bread, or in this case, Matzah, to go along with us.

All speak:

1   **TEFILLAT HA'DERECH:**   May it be thy will,
HASHEM, our God and
God of our forefathers
and foremothers, to lead us on a way of peace, and guide and direct us for
peace, so that we may reach the place we will to be at, with wholehearted
life with joy and with peace. And save us from the palm of all enemies, and
all wild animals, and all shadows of the night and from our own self-
generated fears that arise as we are on our path. Send a blessing onto all the
creations and activities of our hands and give us good grace, kindness and
favor in both Thine eyes and in the eyes of all whom we meet.

2   And when next we drink a cup of wine, and it may be that we will be far
apart, let us remember the four cups of Passover wine, and allow ourselves
to be brought back in our hearts and in our minds, to this night, and this
place and these people, to this Passover Seder, this celebration of liberation,
of **BEING** and **ASKING** and **DOING** and **TRUSTING** and **LETTING GO**, of
rebirth and new beginnings. And till our paths cross once again, Godspeed
my friends.

ACKNOWLEDGMENTS

I received an amazing amount of input, support, and encouragement in creating this book. Several people 'said the right words' or provided the right form of input or encouragement just when I needed it. I want to thank them: my father, Jack Rosenfeld; my teachers, Reb Zalman Schachter-Shalomi and Reb Levi Horowitz; my cousin, David Gold; my former coach, Laurie Green; my personal friends - Marrey Embers, Nancy Haft, Shira Shamssian Israel, Ethel Herring, Yochanan and Mary Francis Kalischer, Brian Goldman and the 'family' at Esalen Institute; and, my professional friends - Andrea Carter, Jon Peck and Dan Spelce.

Several people 'said the right words,' provided the right encouragement AND also reviewed and provided editorial comment to the Haggadah: my brother, Dr. Alvin Rosenfeld, and my friends - Dr. Eleonor Finkelstein, Nancy Abrams, Esq., Miriam Vilozney, Rick Doblin, and Cara Lieb.

And four people 'said the right words,' provided the right encouragement, reviewed and provided editorial comment AND absolutely and completely made this Haggadah possible:

my sister,
Sheila Rosenfeld Zucker
my brother-by-choice,
Dr. Ed Whitney
my computer design/typesetter,
Paula Spencer
and my artist,
Nina Paley

Without them, and the will of HASHEM, there is no way this Haggadah would have happened.

(Special thanks to Alisa Woods, graphic desginer, for jumping in at the last minute and doing paste-up of the Hebrew calligraphy.)